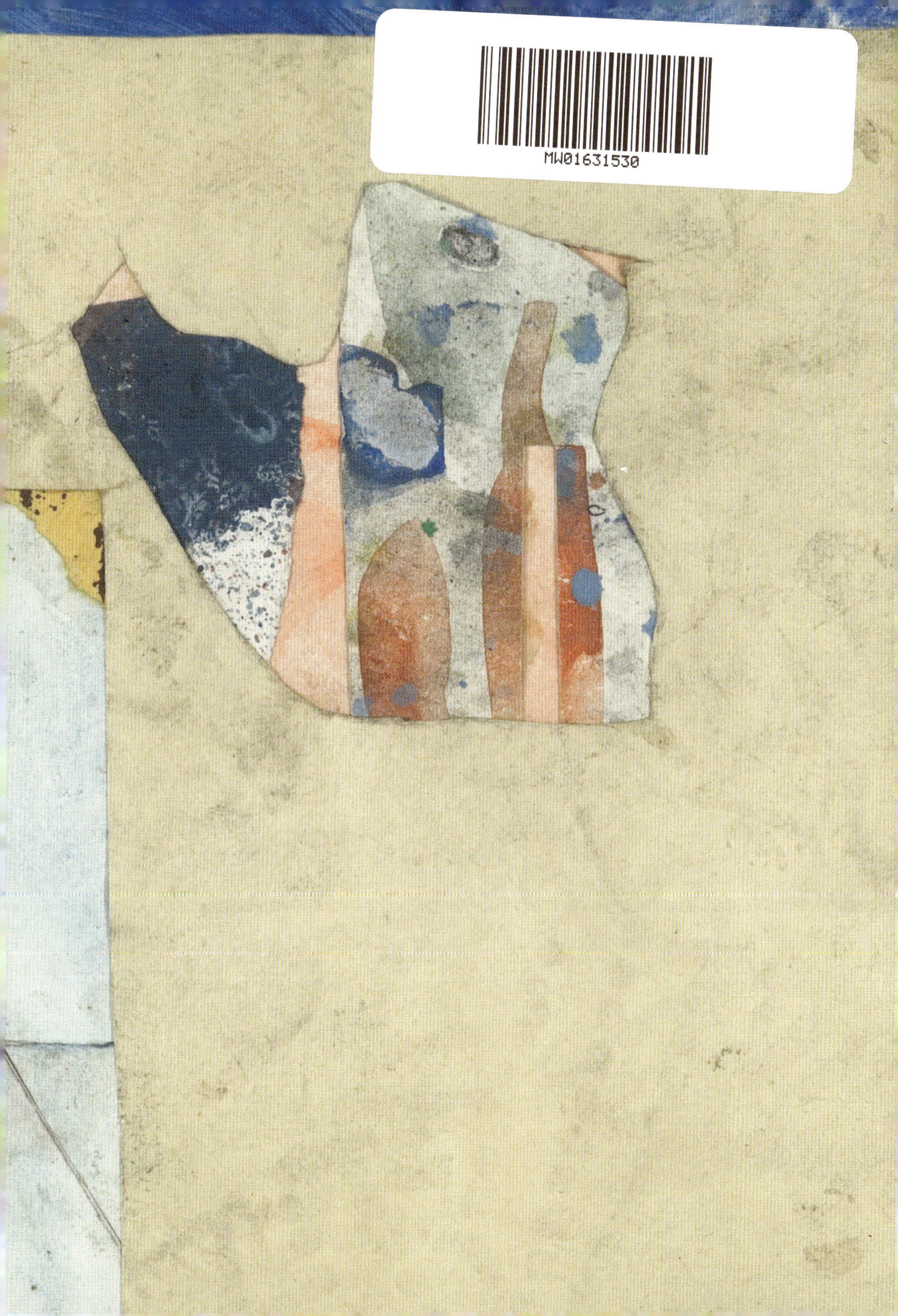
MW01631530

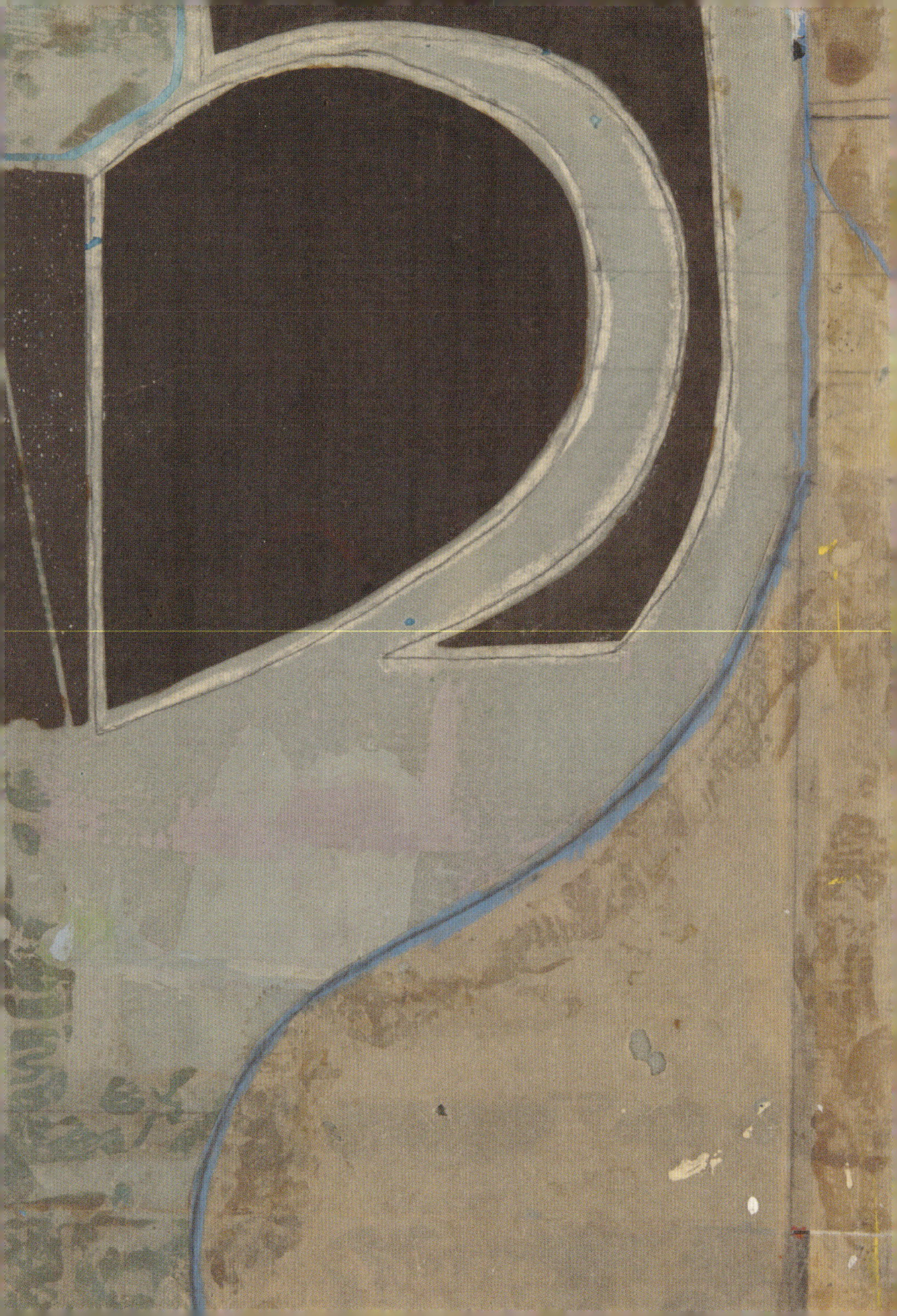

ABSTRACTIONS ON PAPER

RICHARD DIEBENKORN

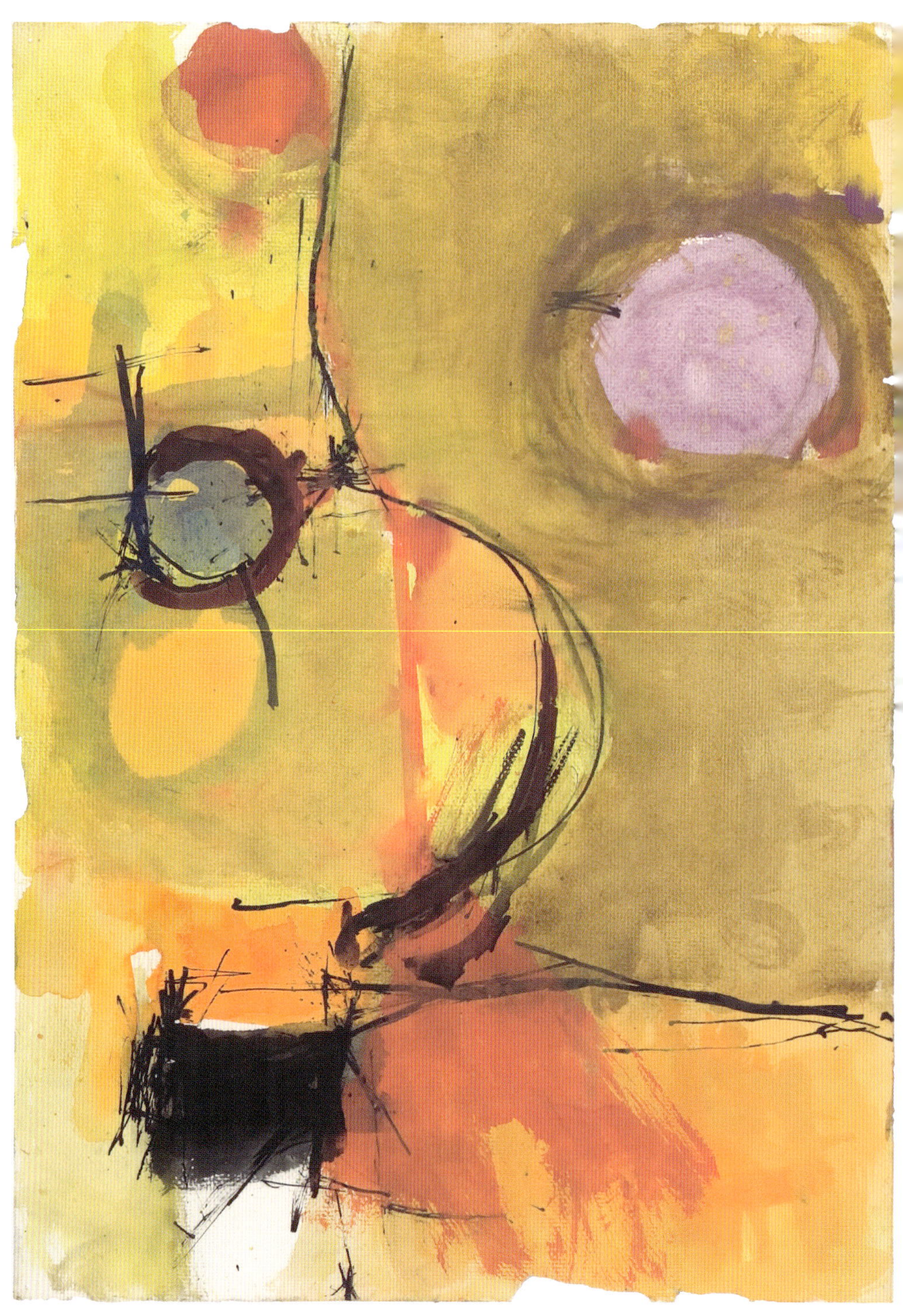

ABSTRACTIONS ON PAPER

RICHARD DIEBENKORN

Edited by Bart Schneider

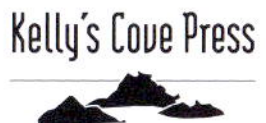

Published by Kelly's Cove Press

2733 Prince Street

Berkeley, CA 94705

www.kellyscovepress.com

Published in the United States of America

ISBN 978-0-9891664-0-9

Library of Congress Control Number: 2013937029

Third printing, April 2014

Cover and interior design by Robin Ann McIntosh and Vincent Romero

Cover drawing: Richard Diebenkorn, Untitled, 1967/1991

Gouache, crayon, ballpoint pen and graphite on paper

8 3/8 x 8 1/2 in. (21.3 x 21.6 cm)

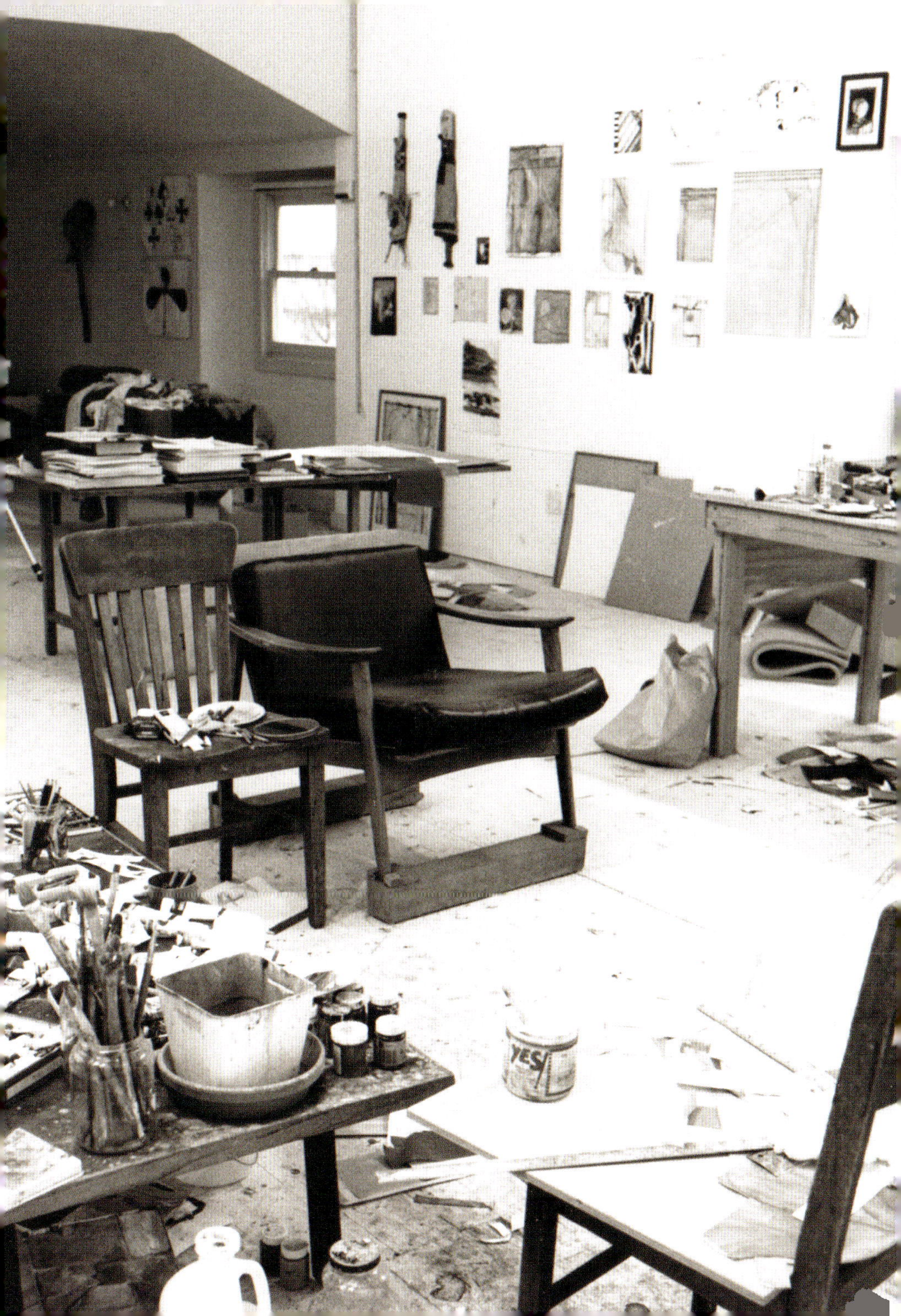
YES!

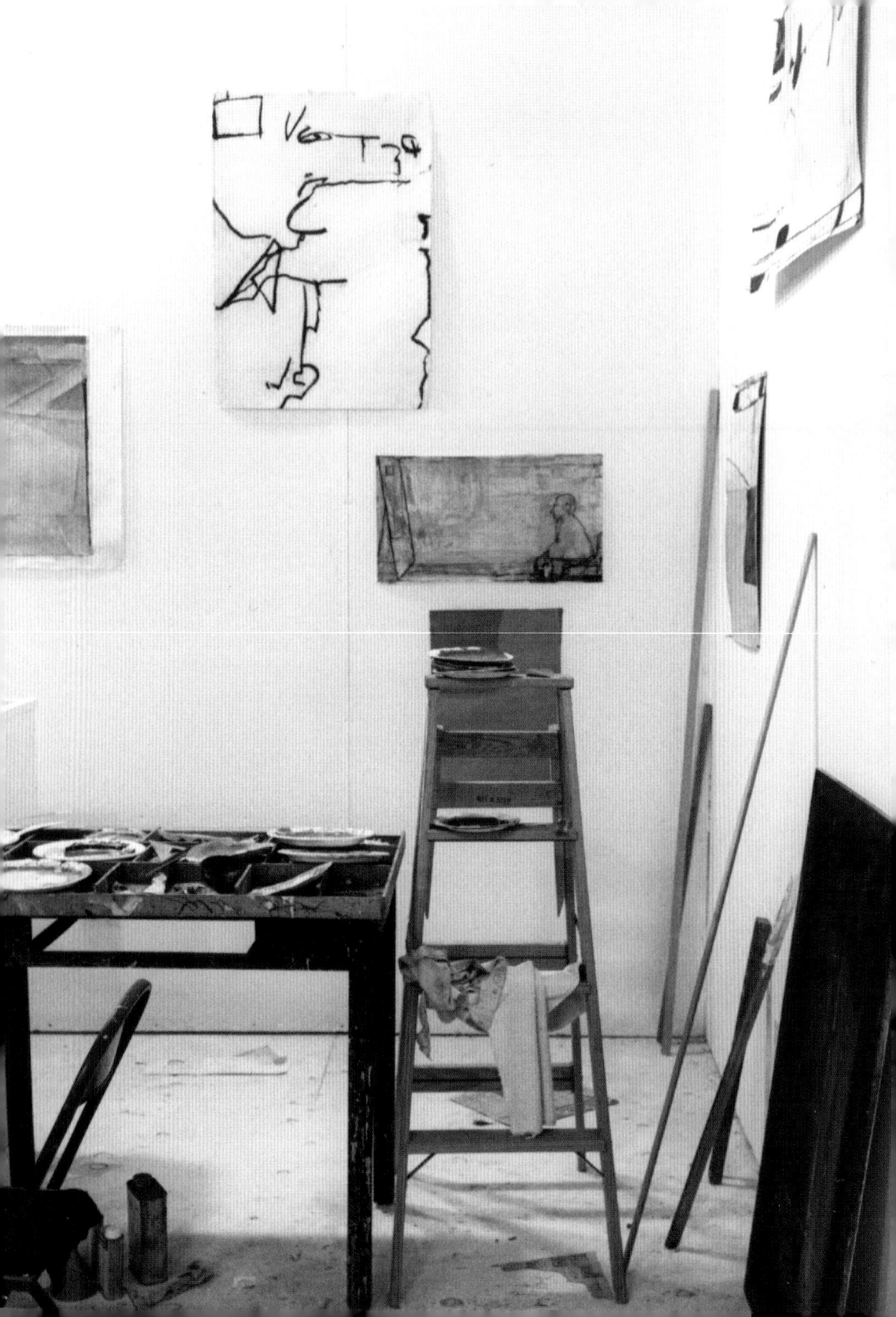

The book is published in connection with an exhibition
of the Richard Diebenkorn Foundation

THE INTIMATE DIEBENKORN: WORKS ON PAPER *1949–1992*

College of Marin Fine Arts Gallery
Kentfield, Calif., September 23 – November 14, 2013

The show will travel to

Natalie & James Thompson Gallery
San José State University
San José, Calif., March 18 – May 16, 2014

Katzen Arts Center
American University
Washington, D.C., November 8 – December 14, 2014

Sonoma Valley Museum of Art
Sonoma, Calif., June 6 – August 23, 2015

Montana Museum of Art & Culture
The University of Montana
Missoula, Mont., September 24 – December 12, 2015

SAUSALITO

ALBUQUERQUE

URBANA

BERKELEY

1949–1955

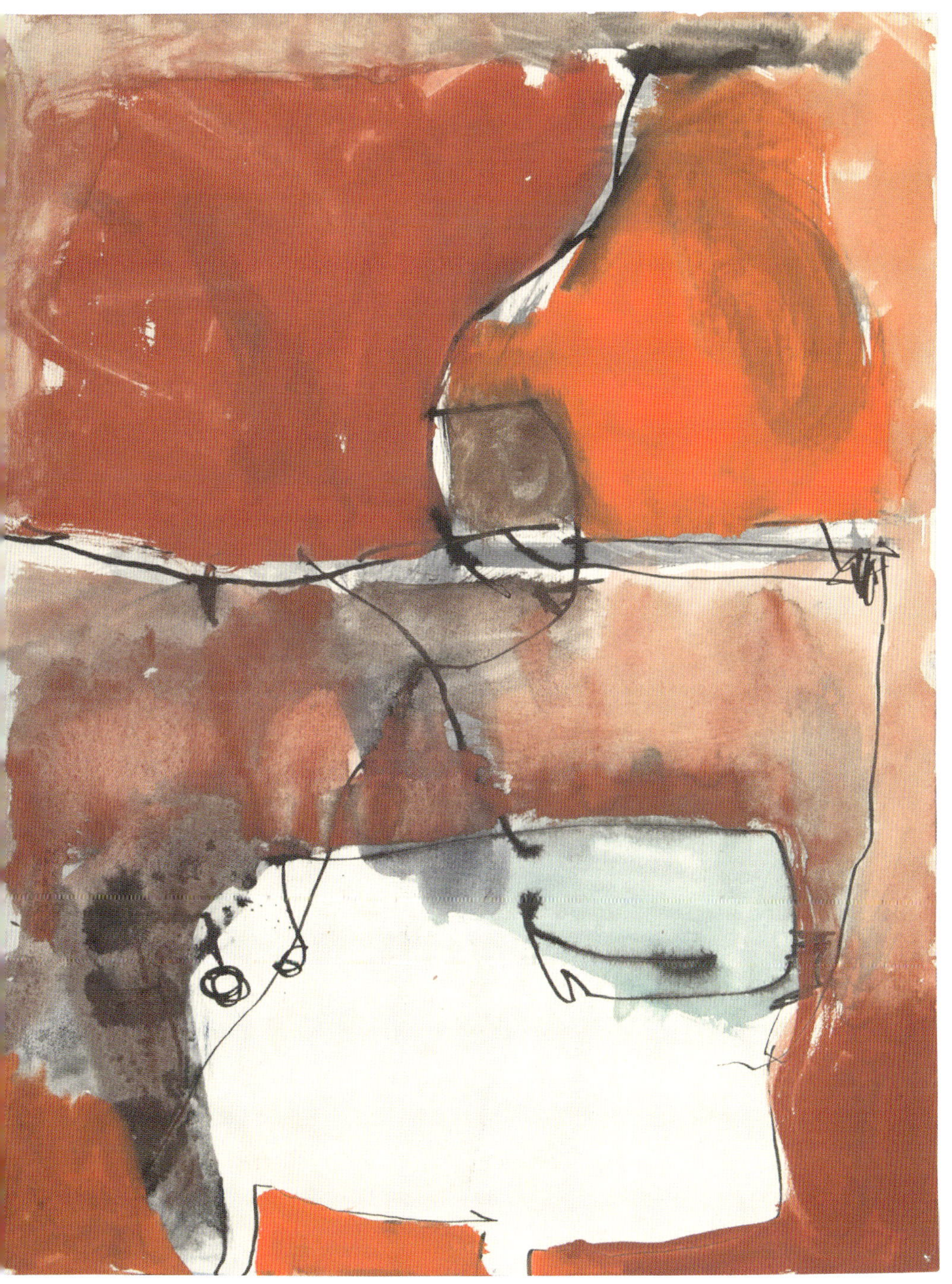

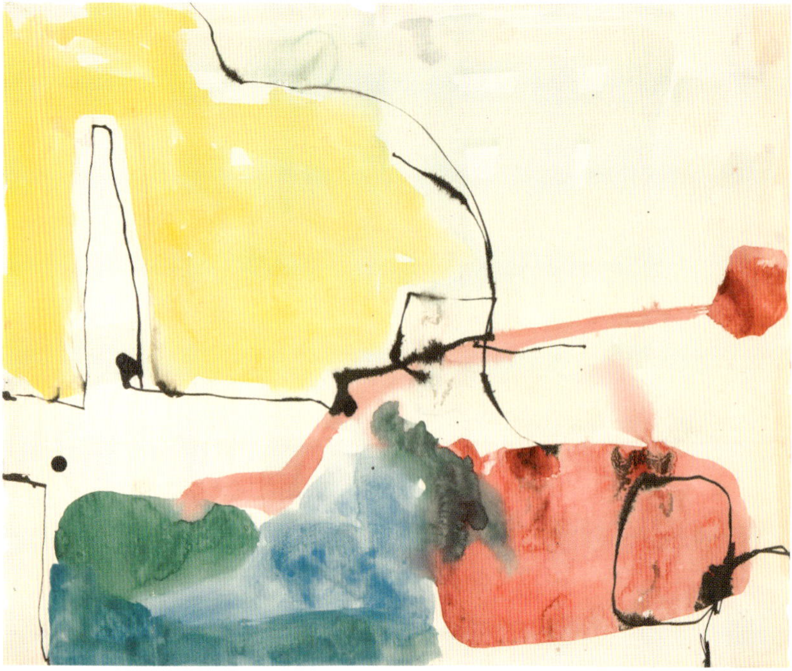

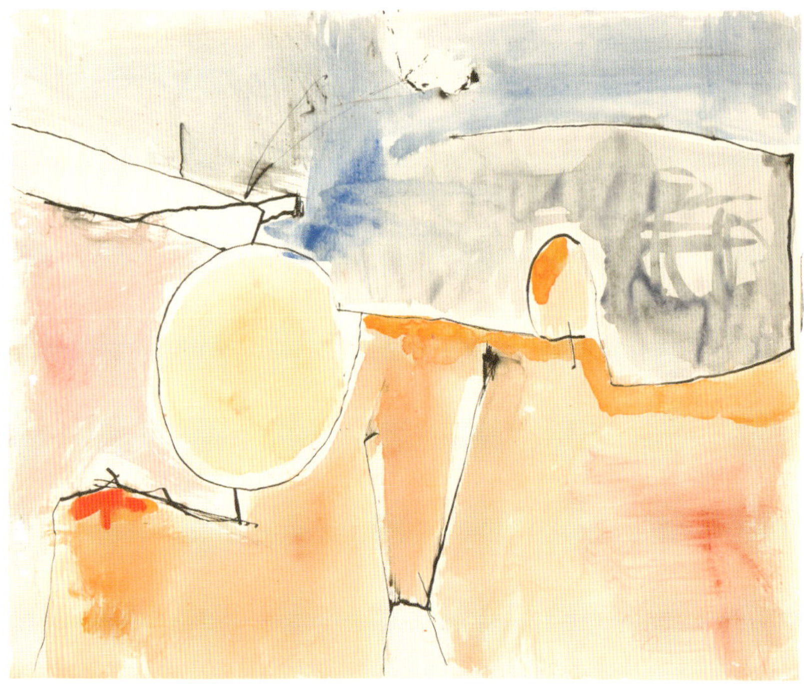

A way is just what I don't want... With each new painting I find a way all too soon, and that's when the trouble starts.

• • • •

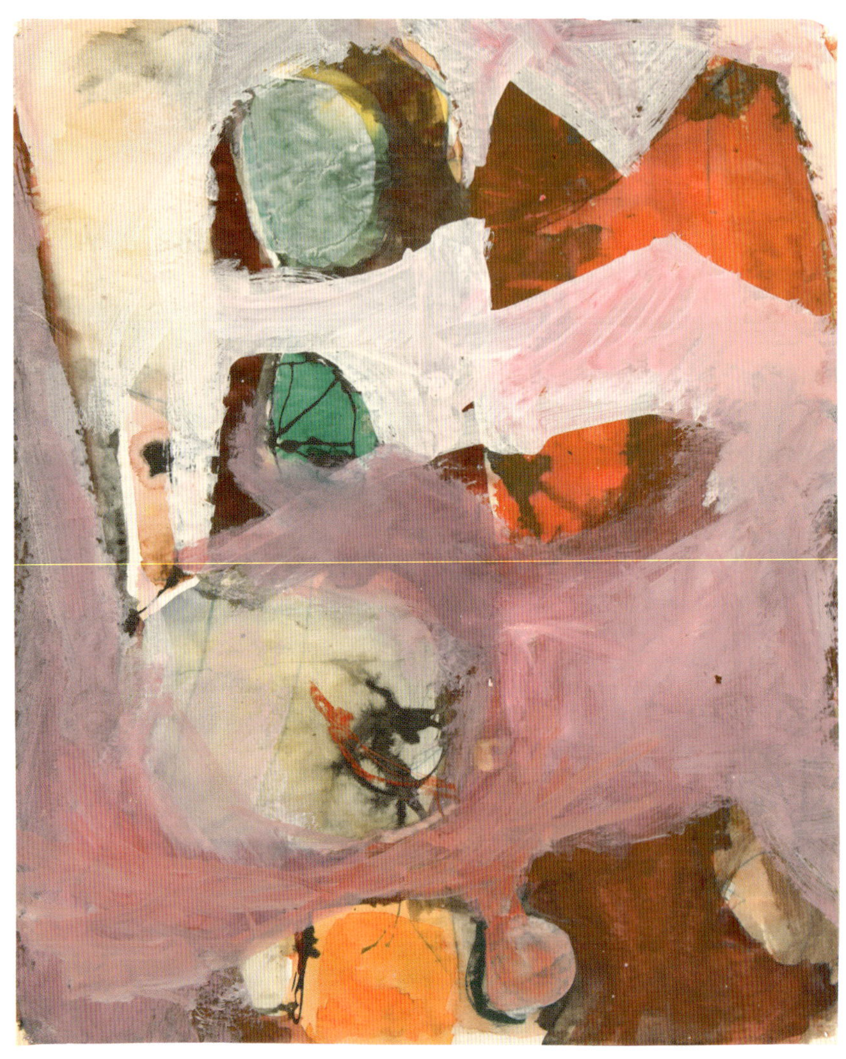

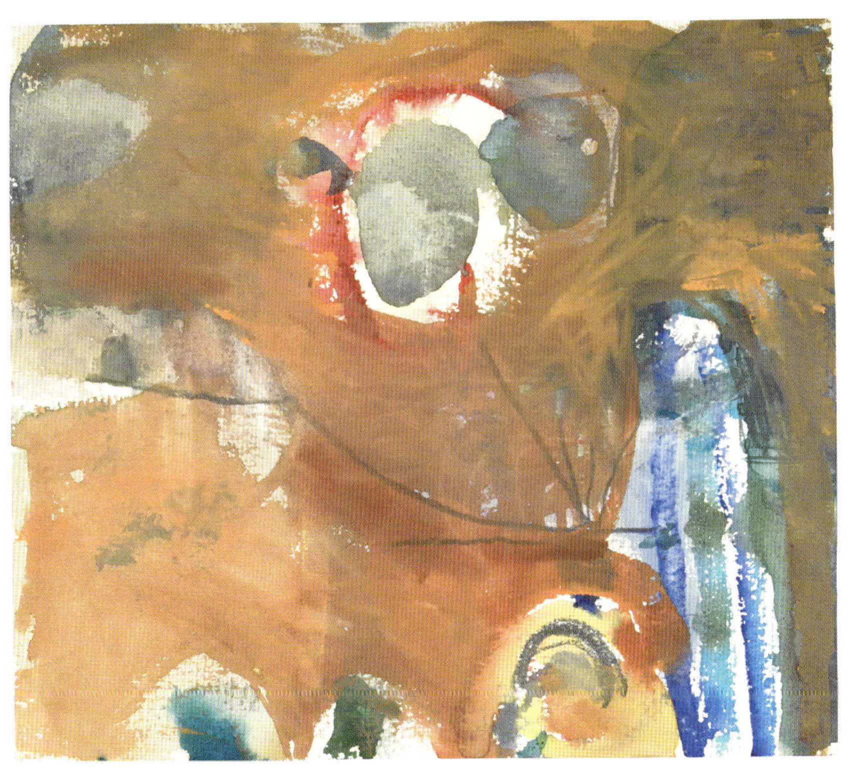

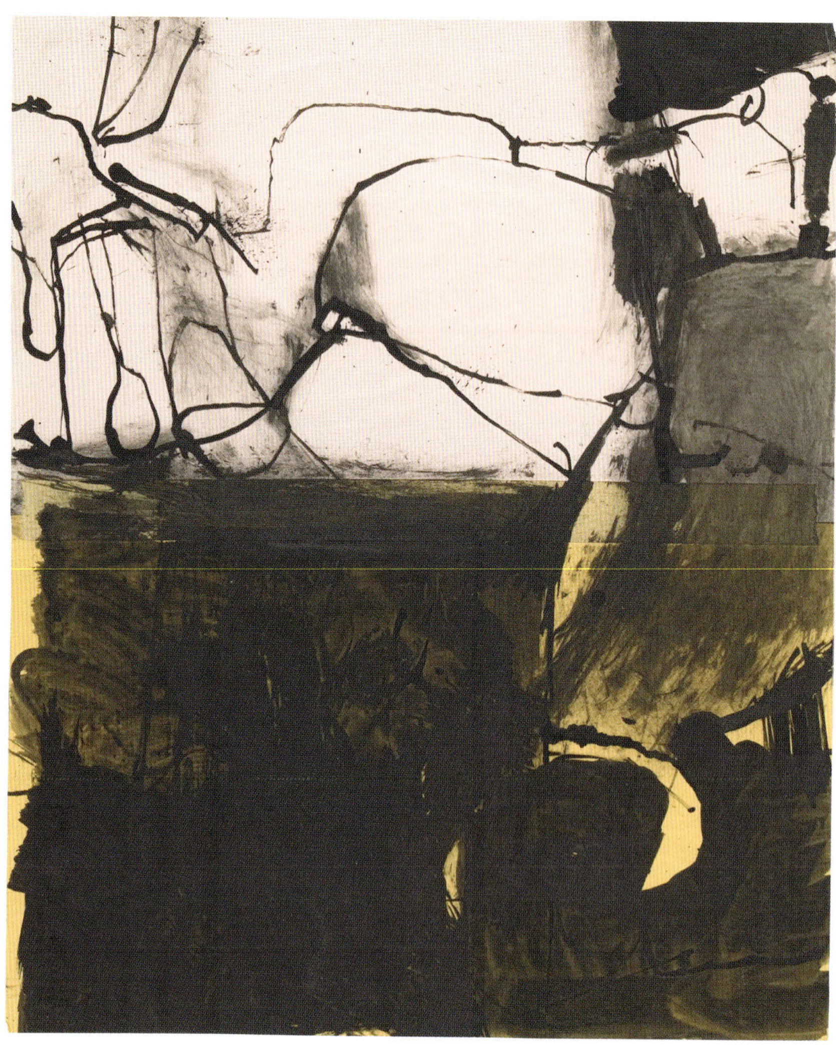

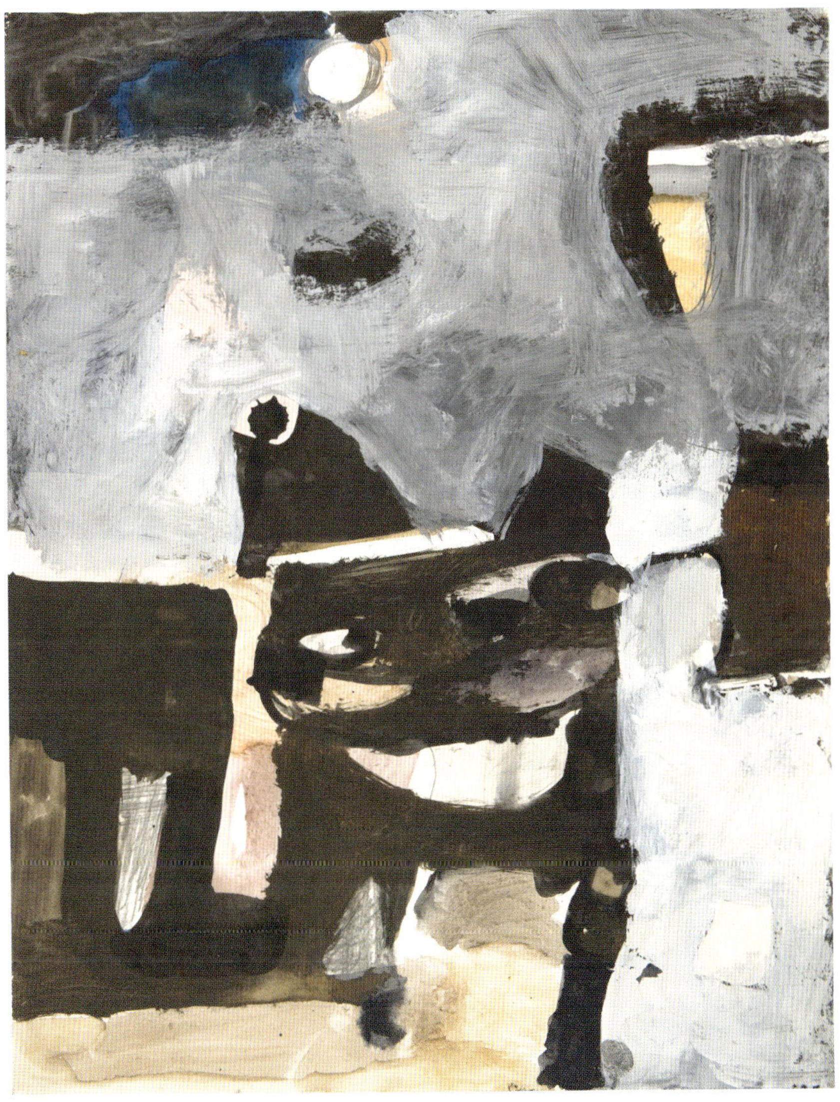

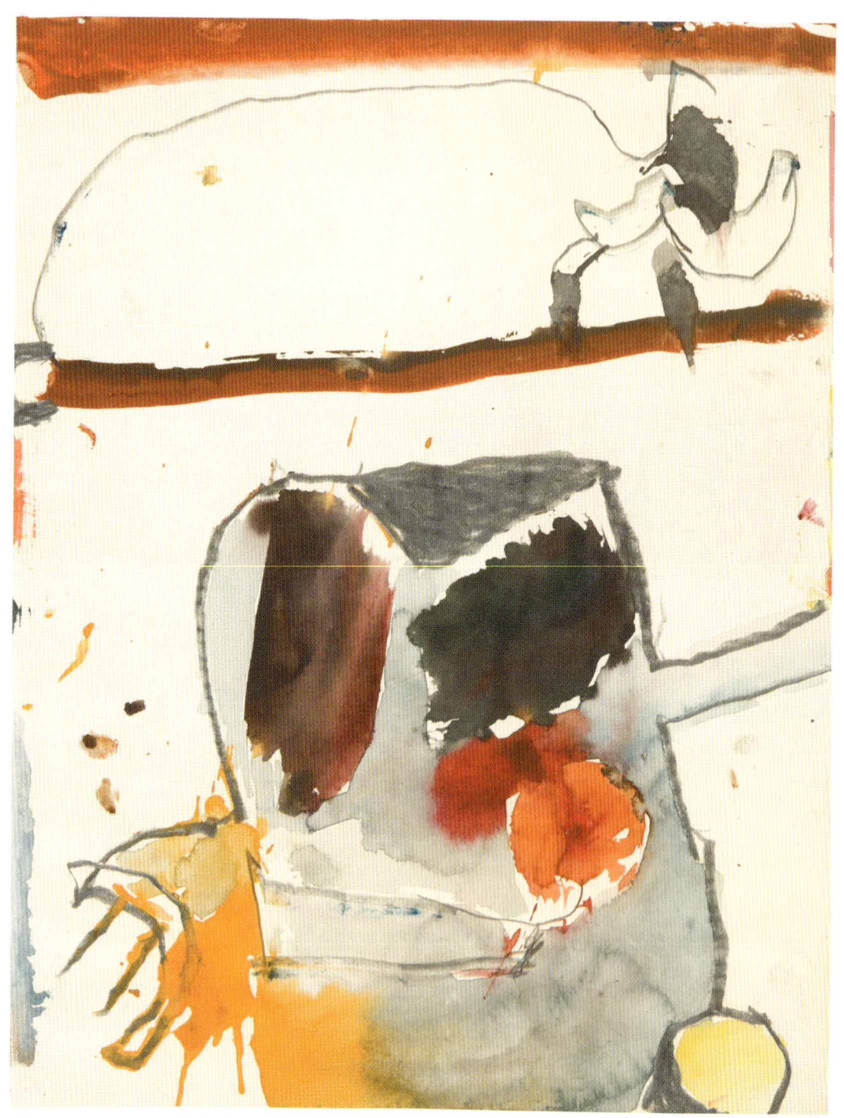

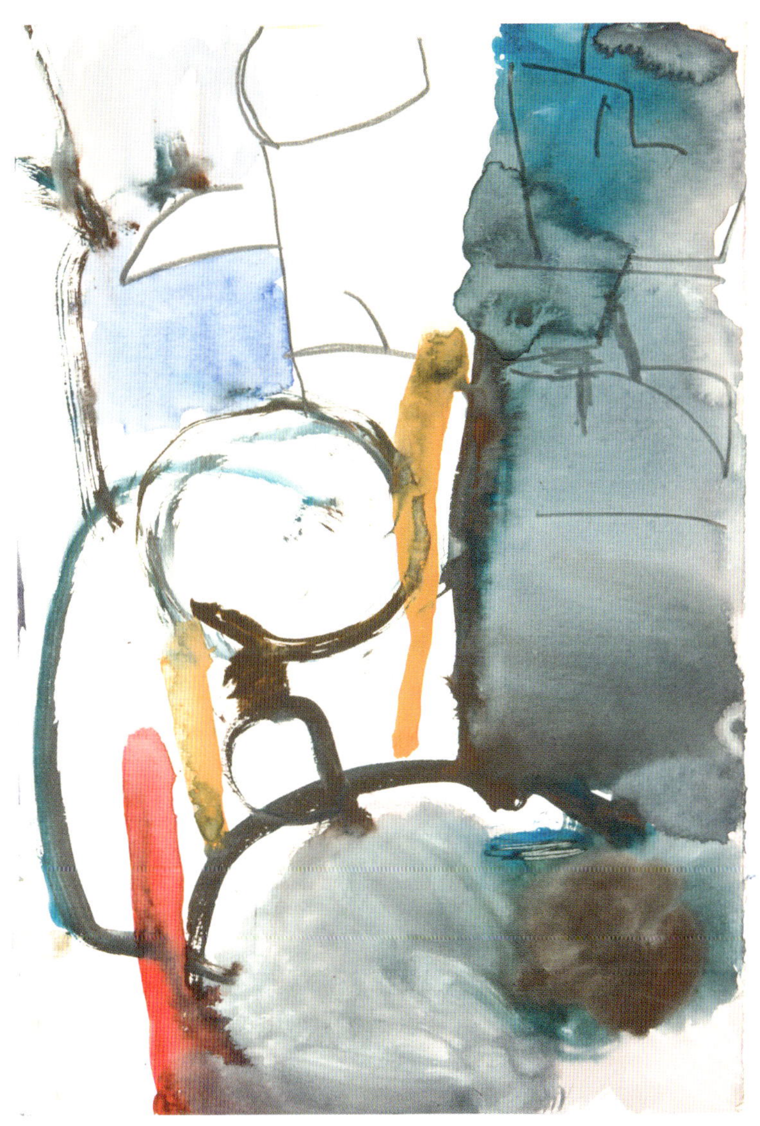

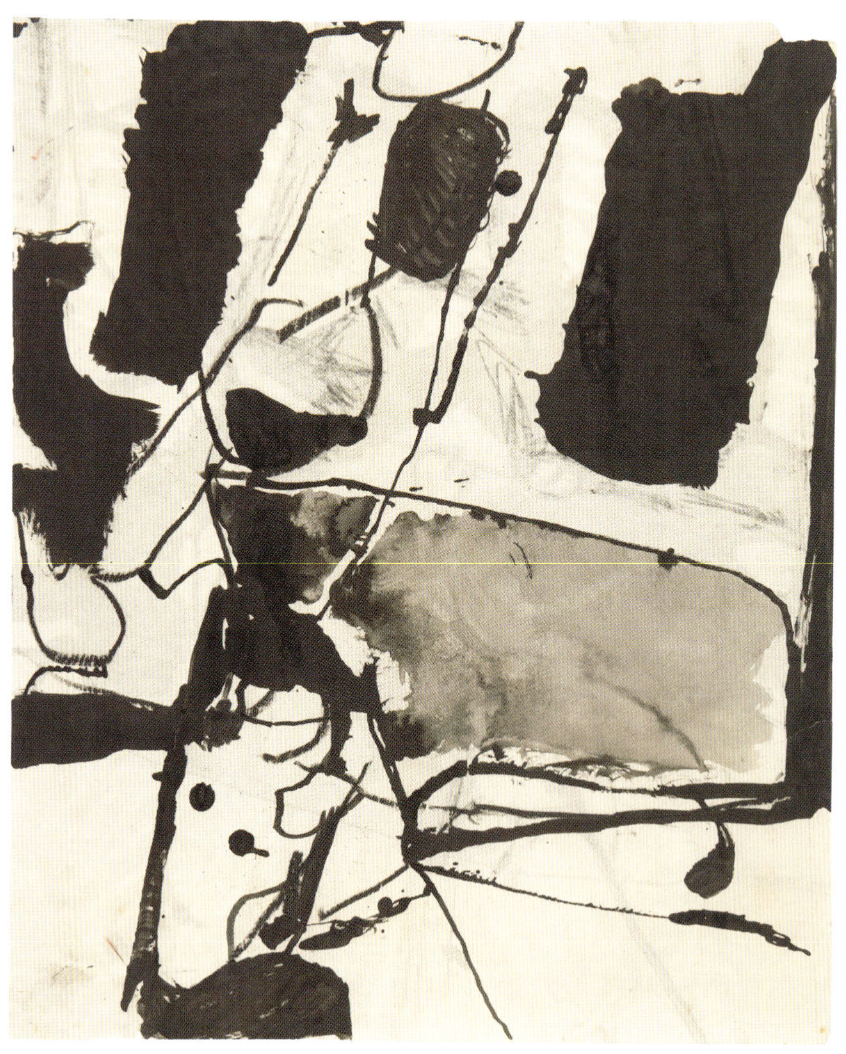

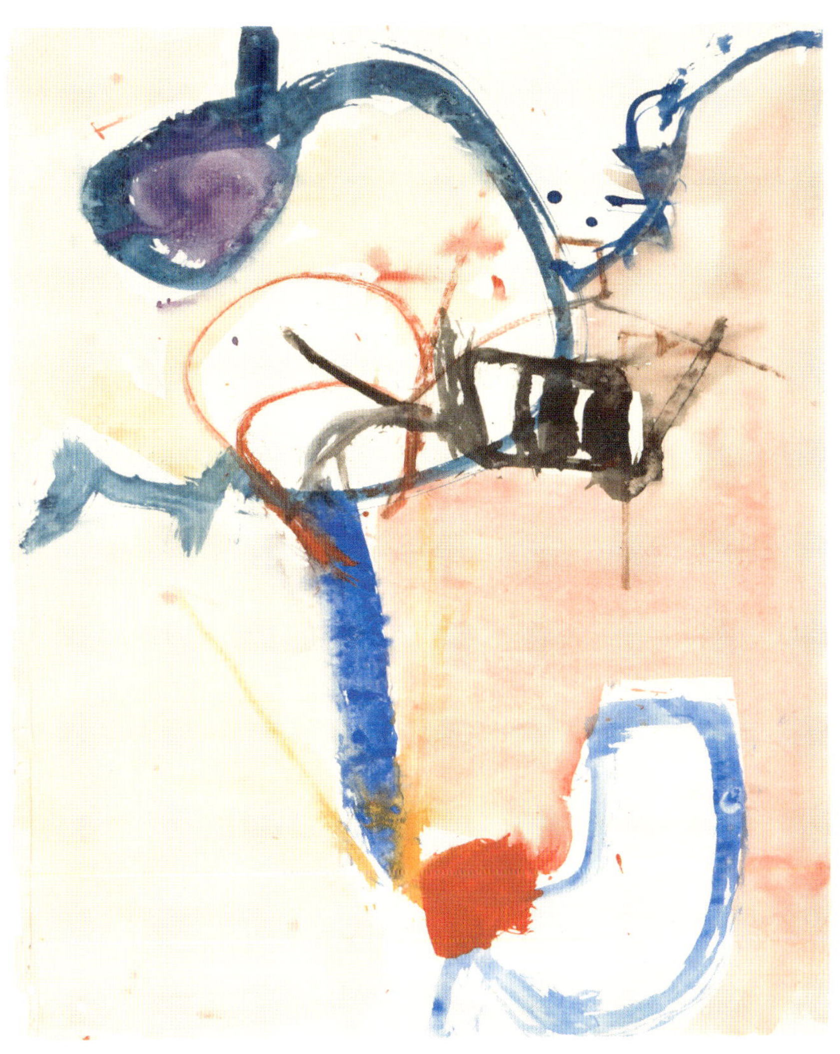

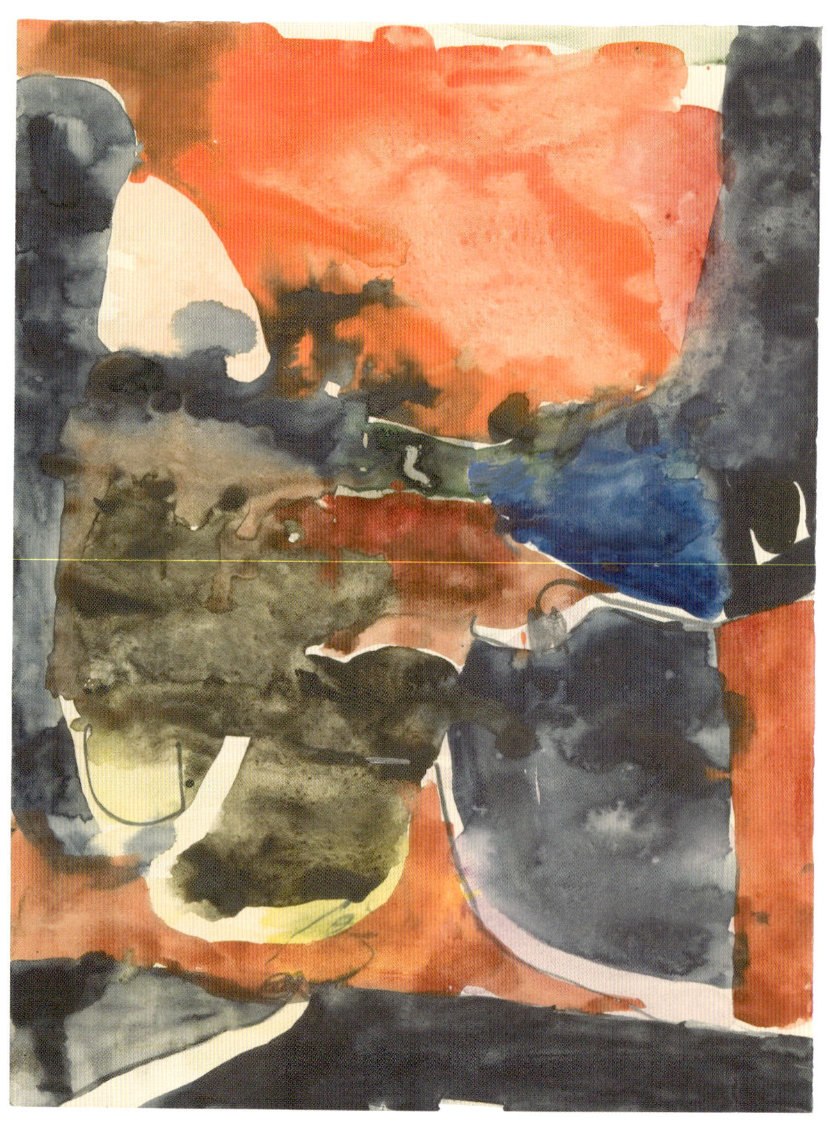

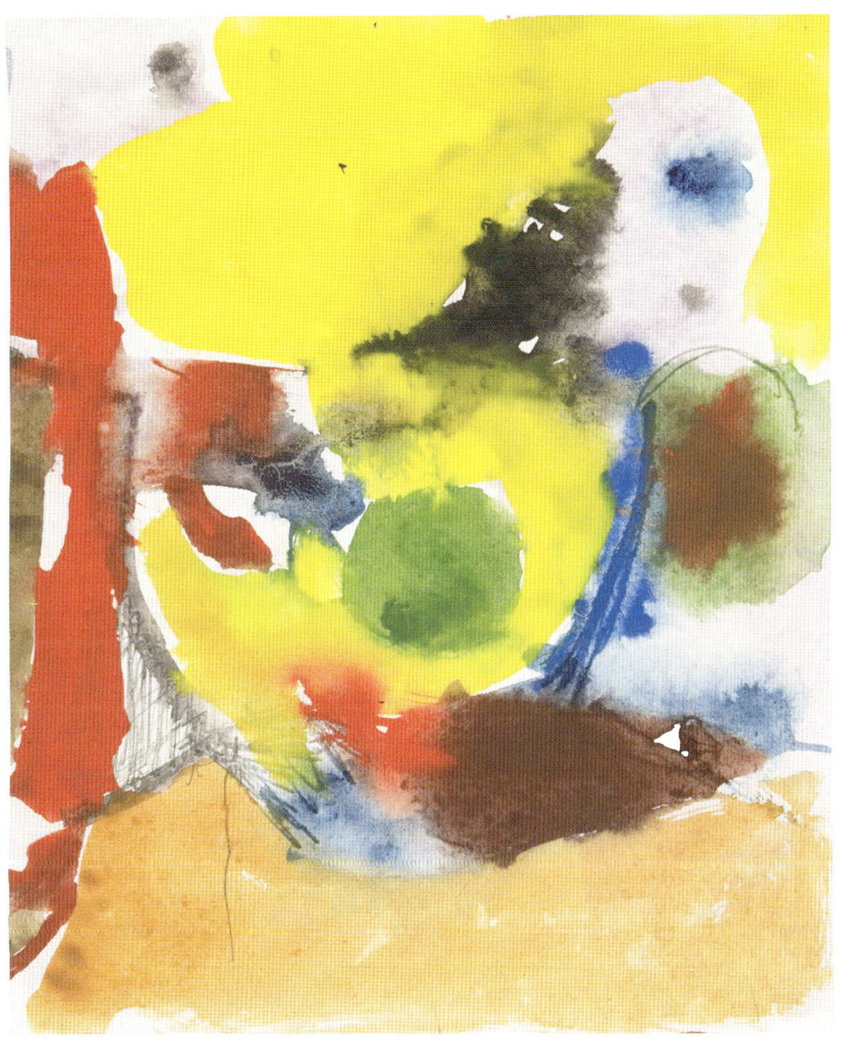

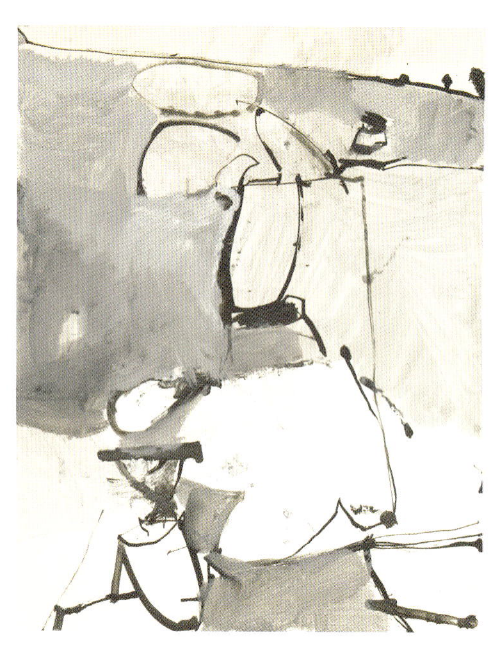

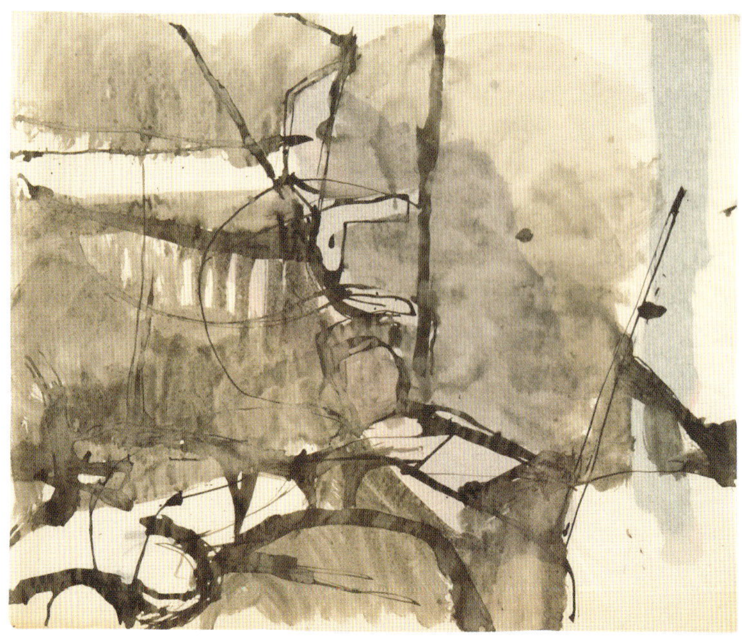

I can never accomplish what I want—only what I would have wanted had I thought of it beforehand.

• • • •

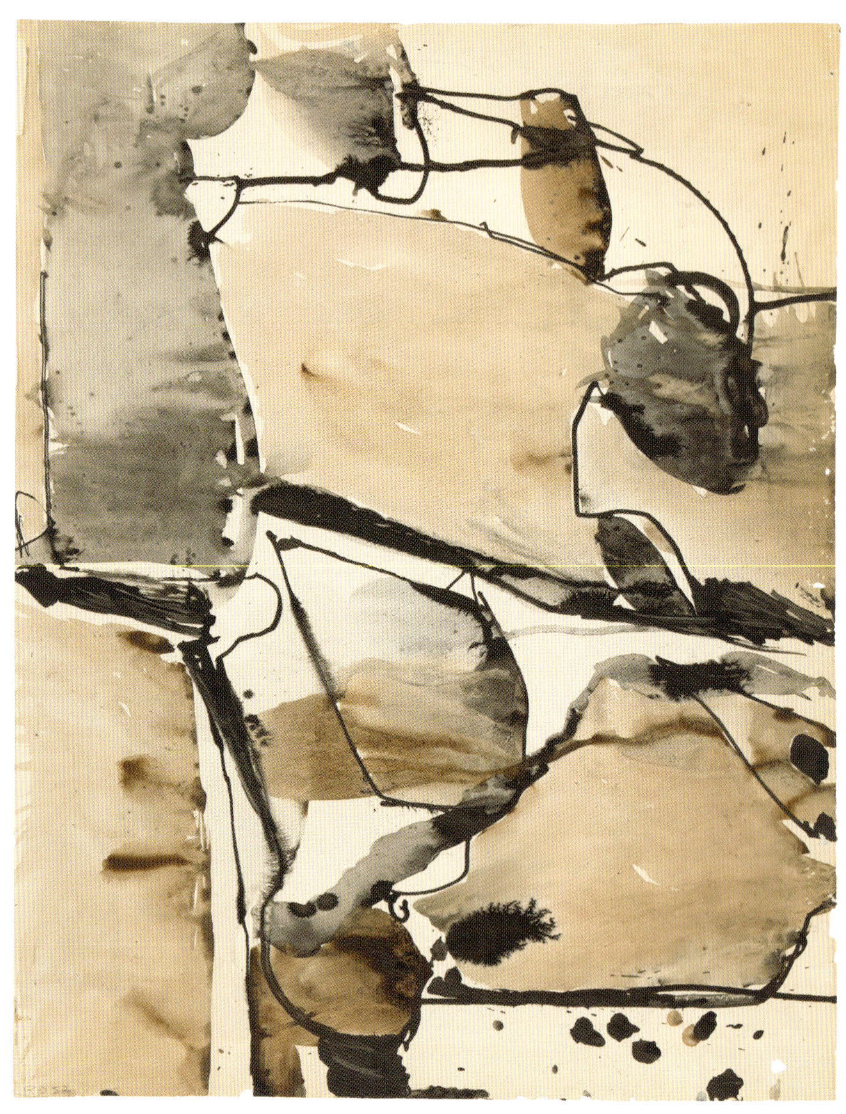

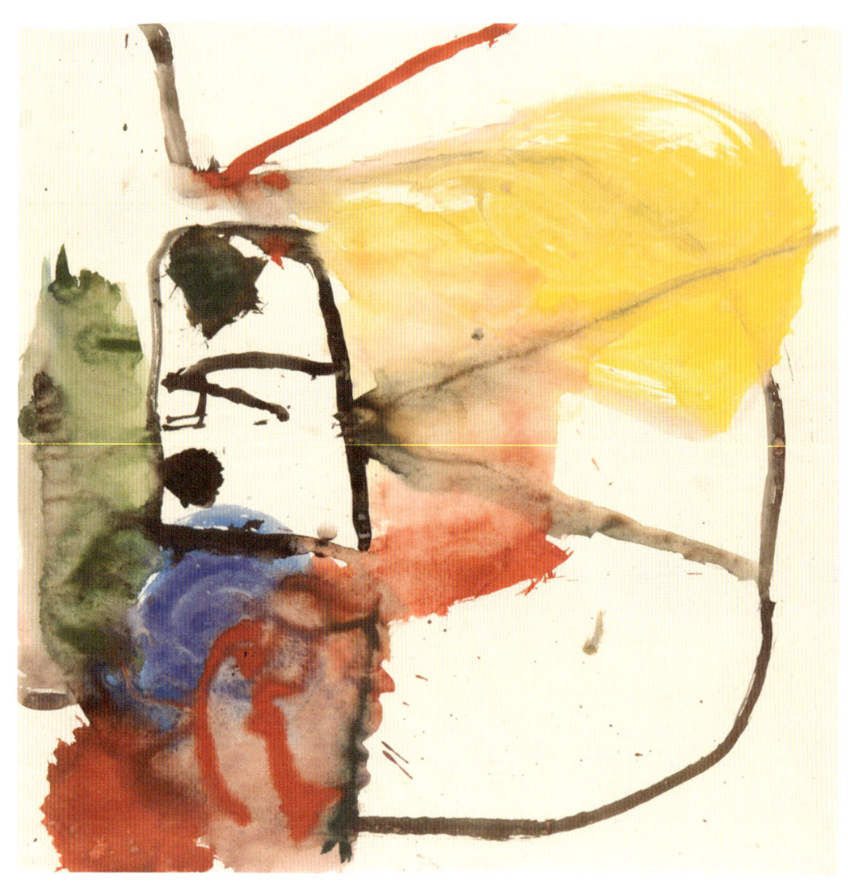

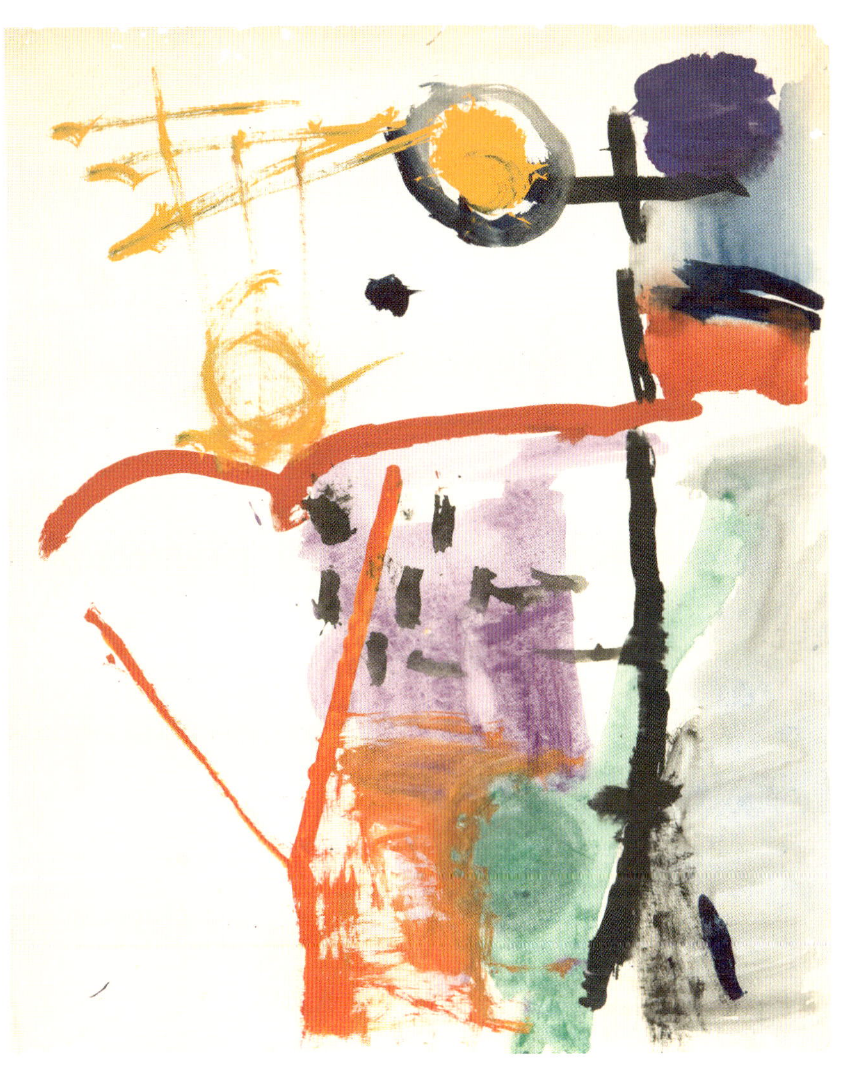

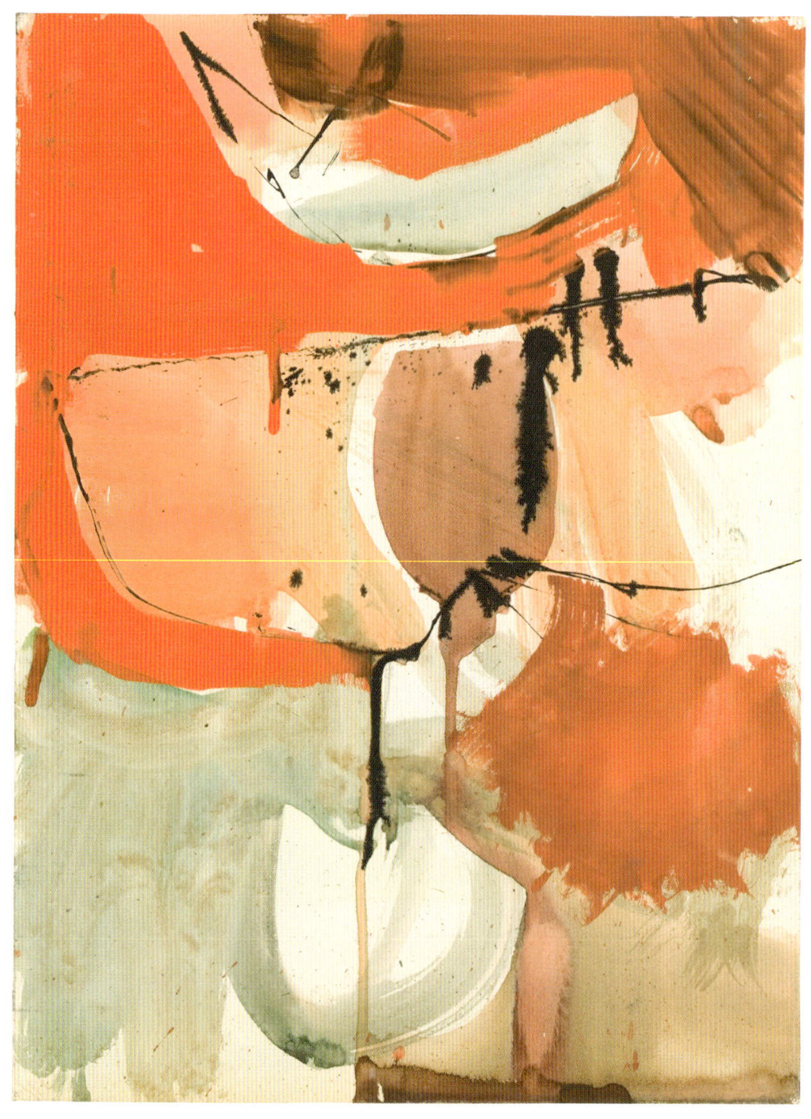

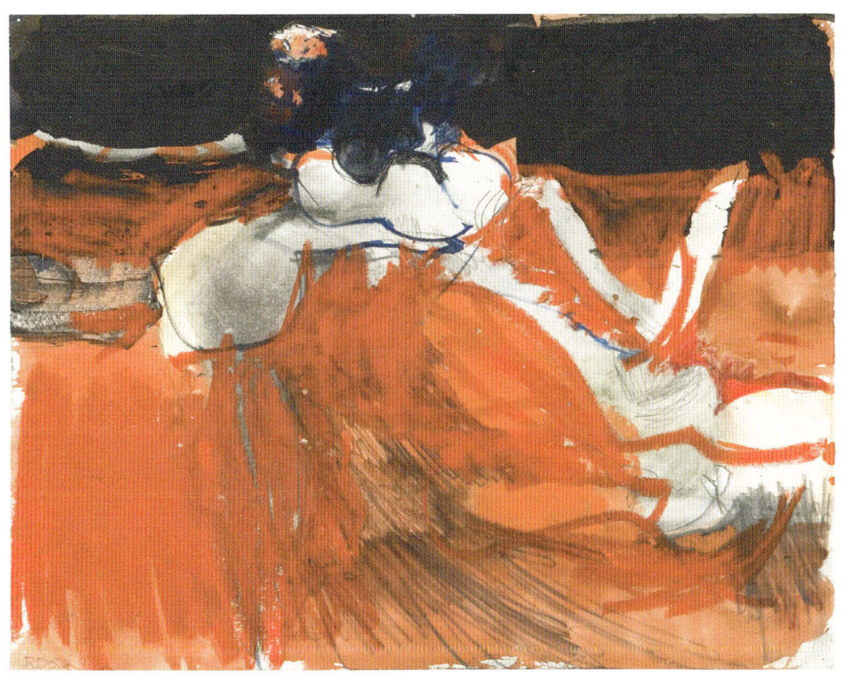

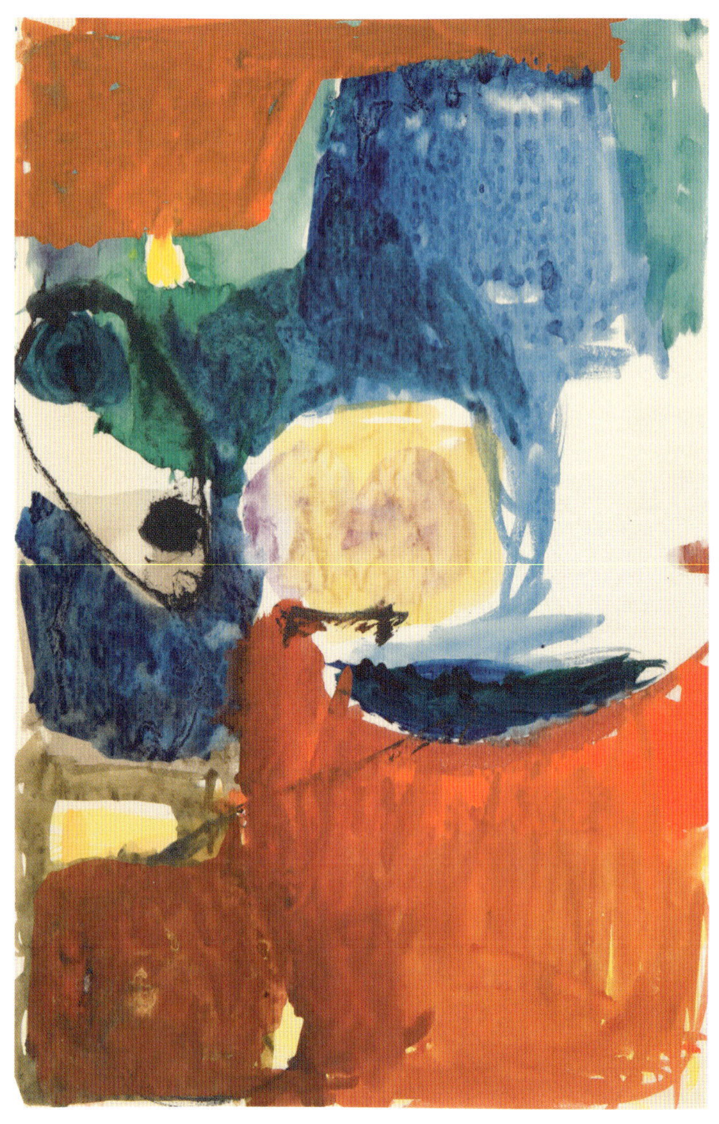

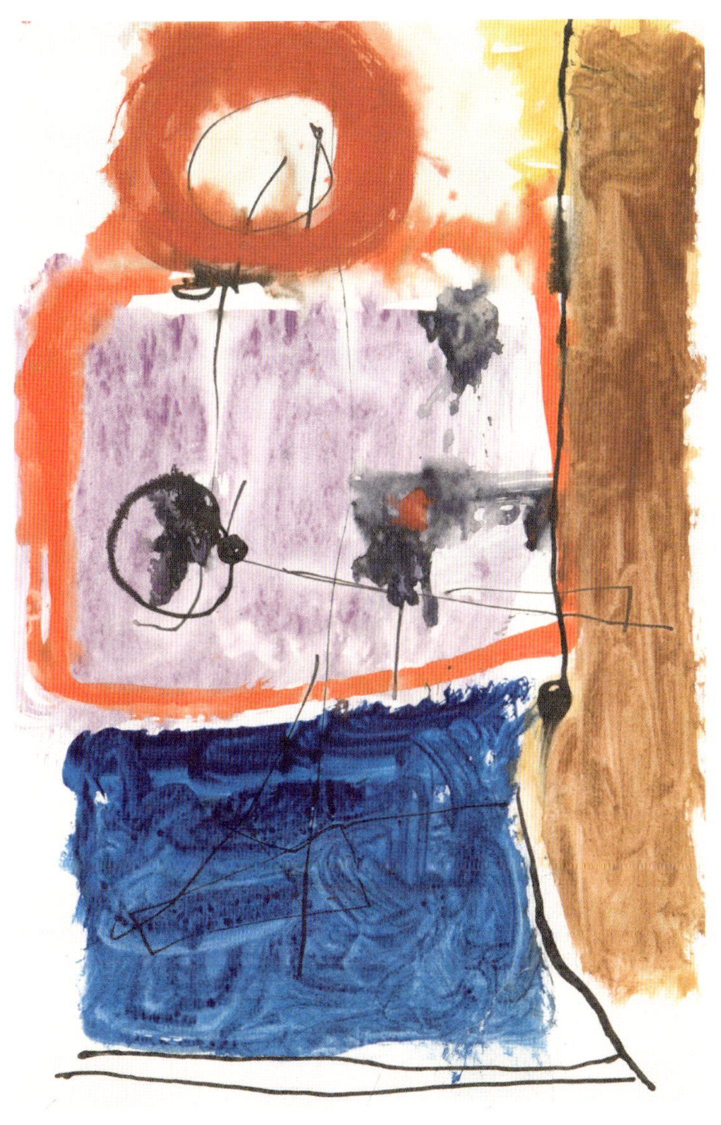

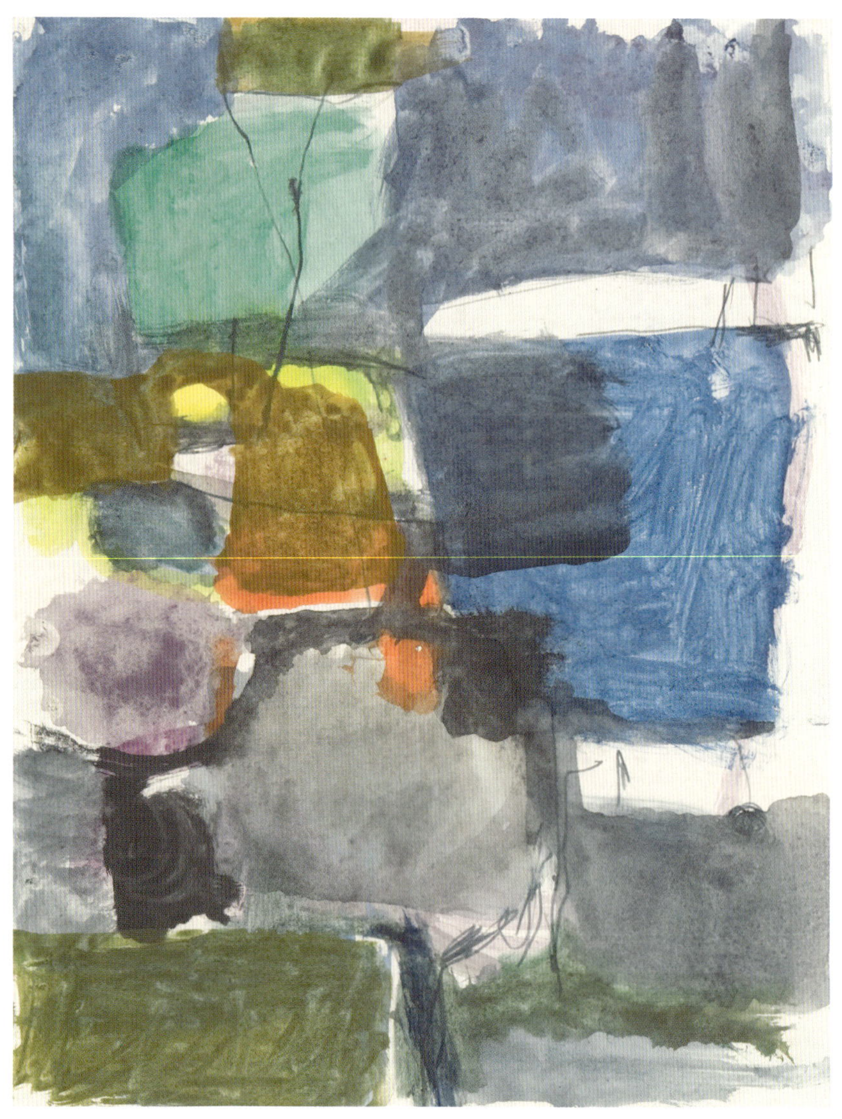

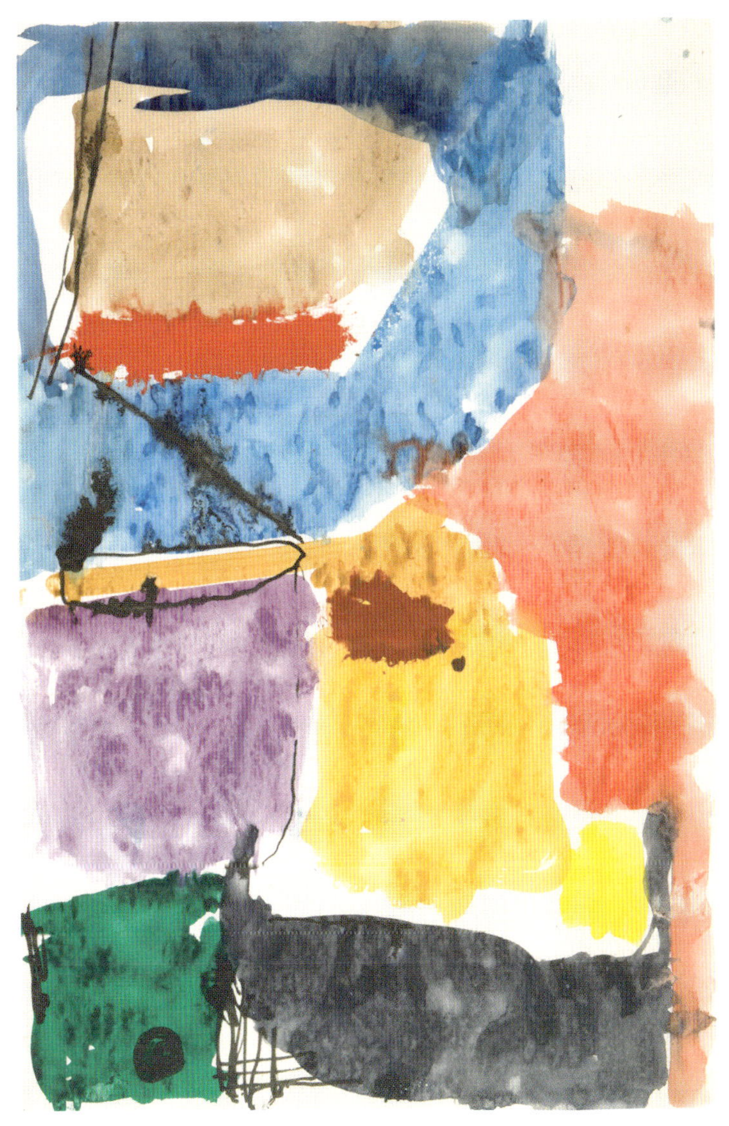

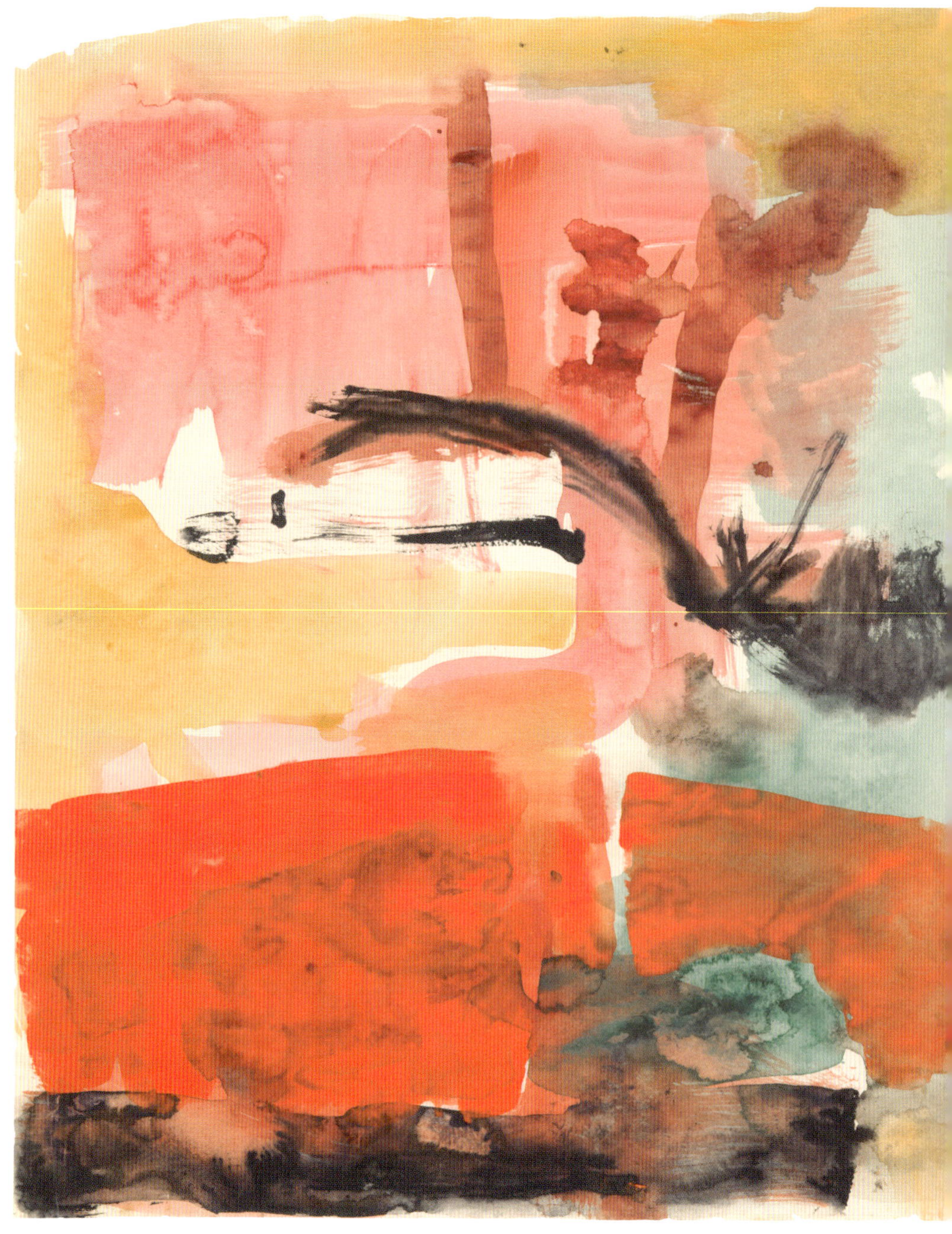

It wasn't art that I was interested in; it was drawing and painting... I had no real understanding of drawing and painting as art.

* * * *

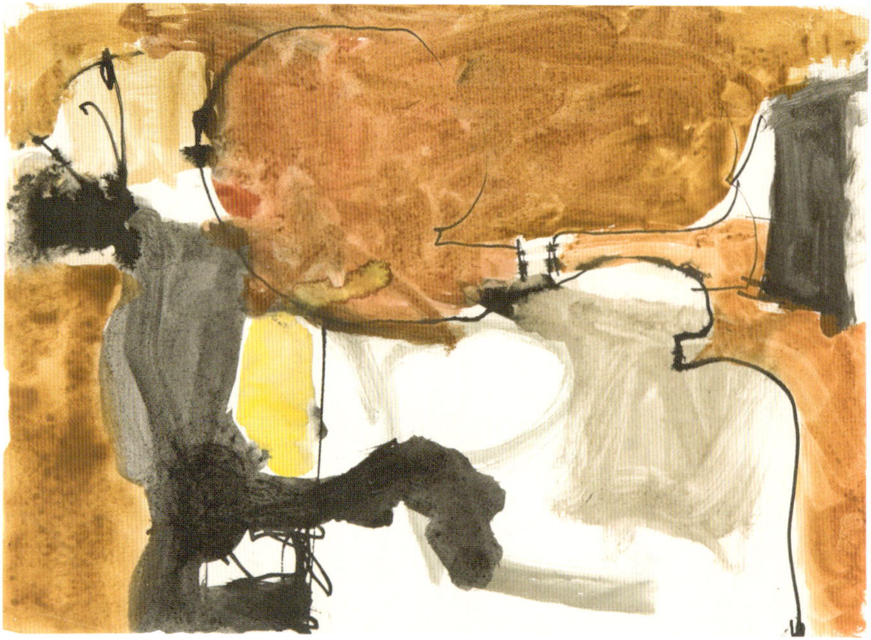

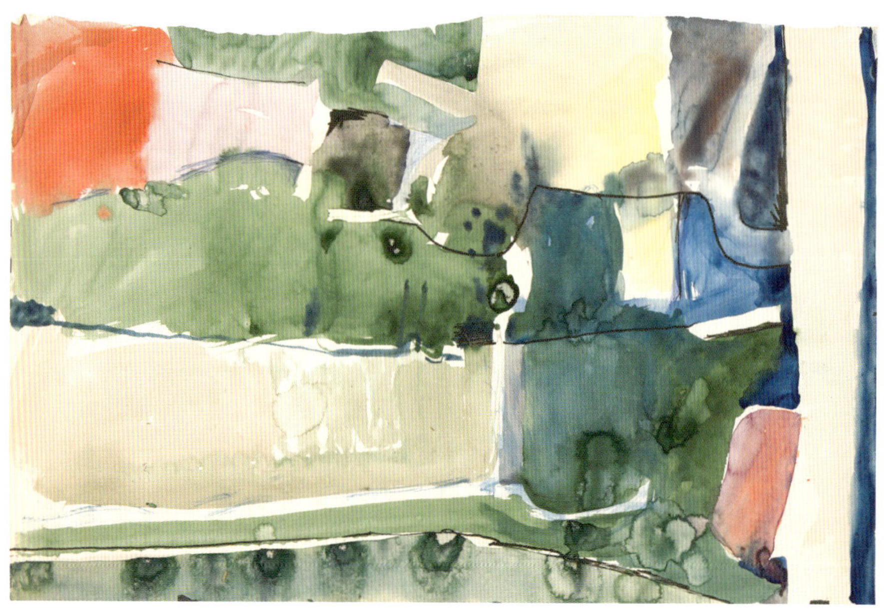

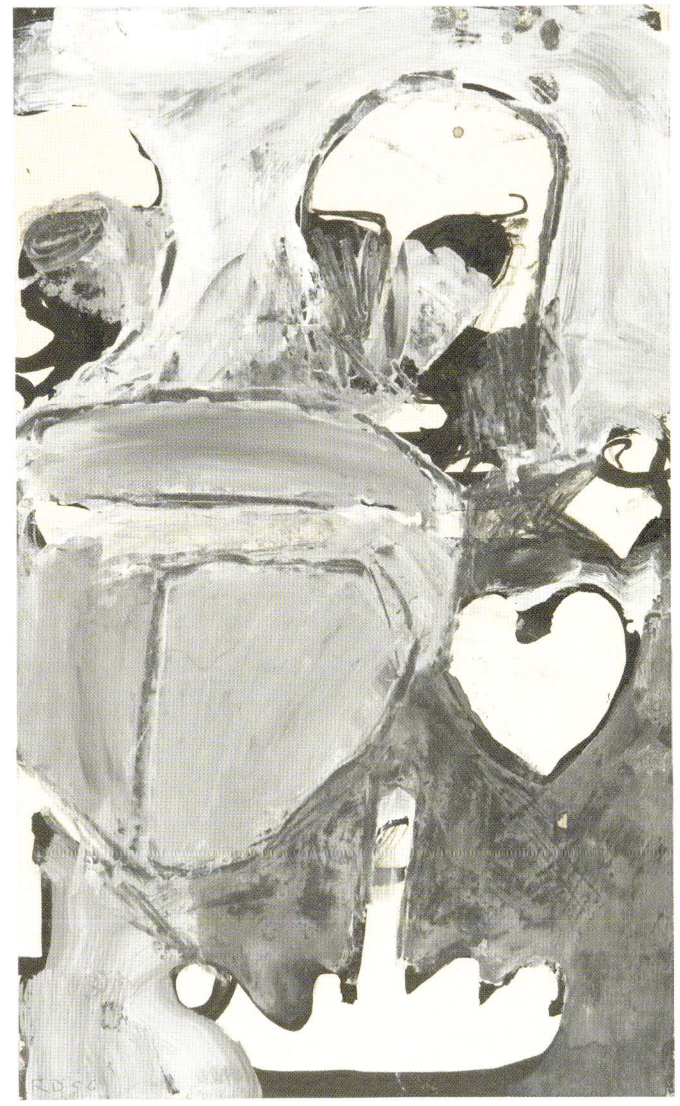

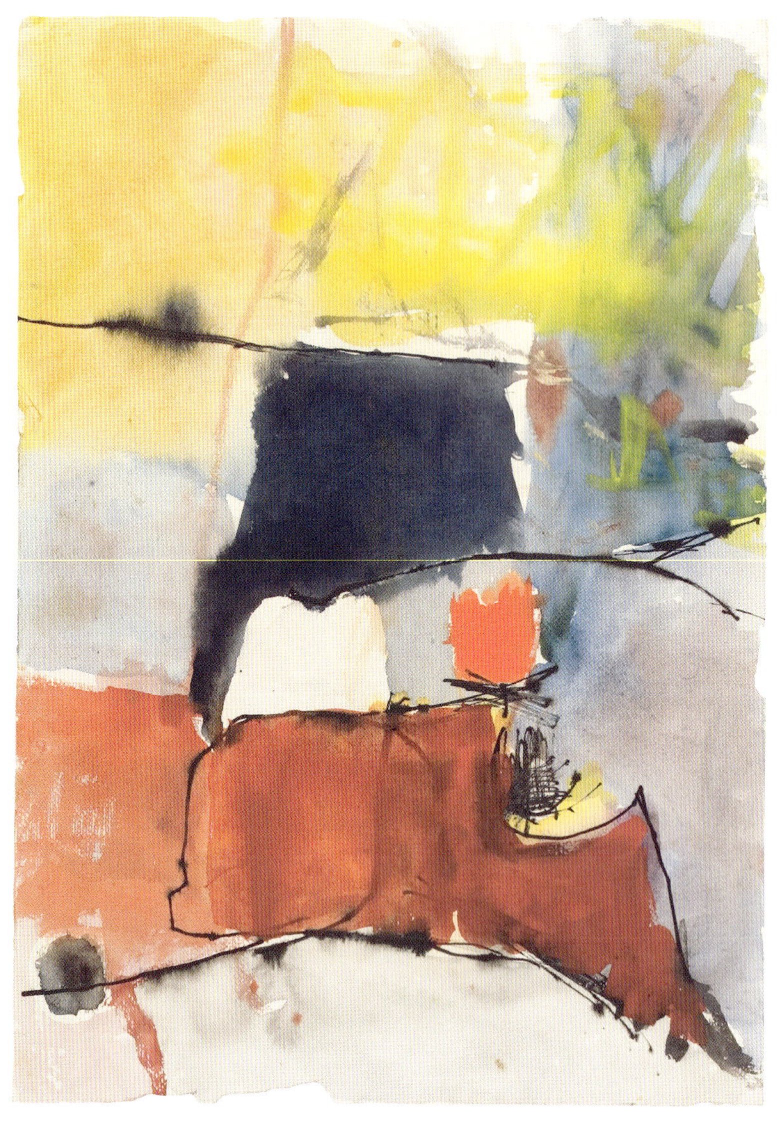

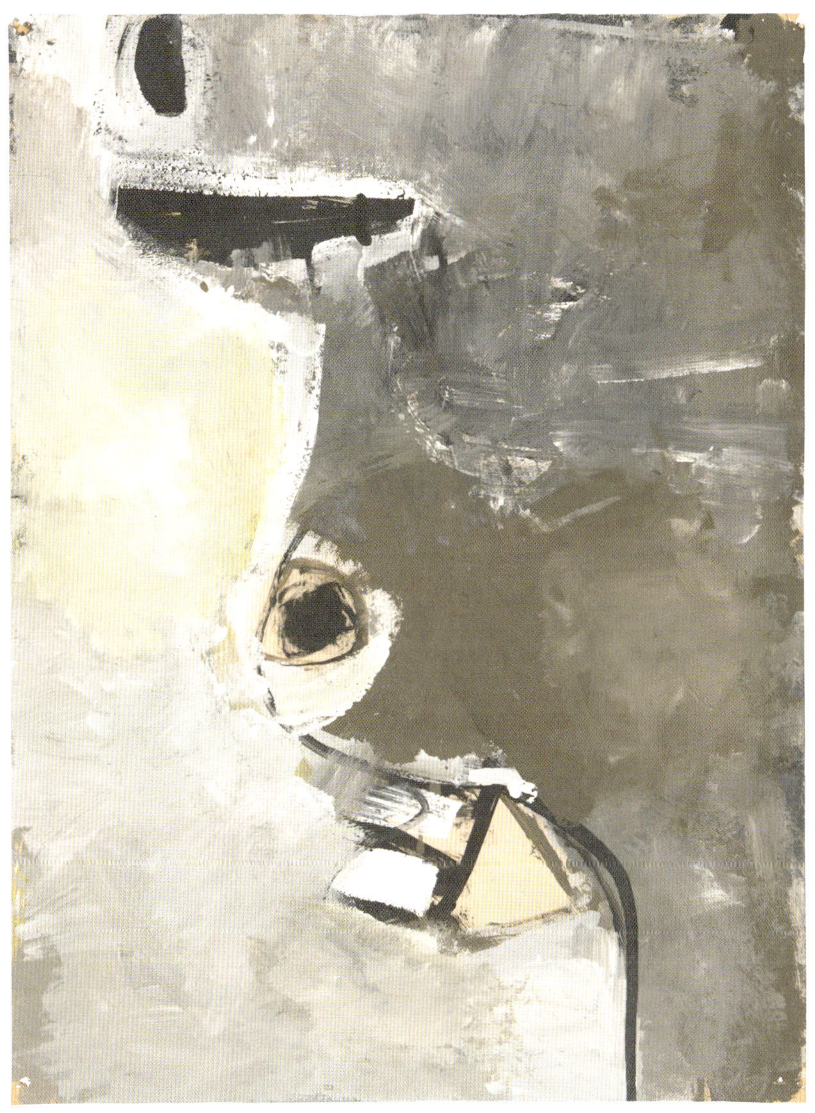

OCEAN PARK

1967–1988

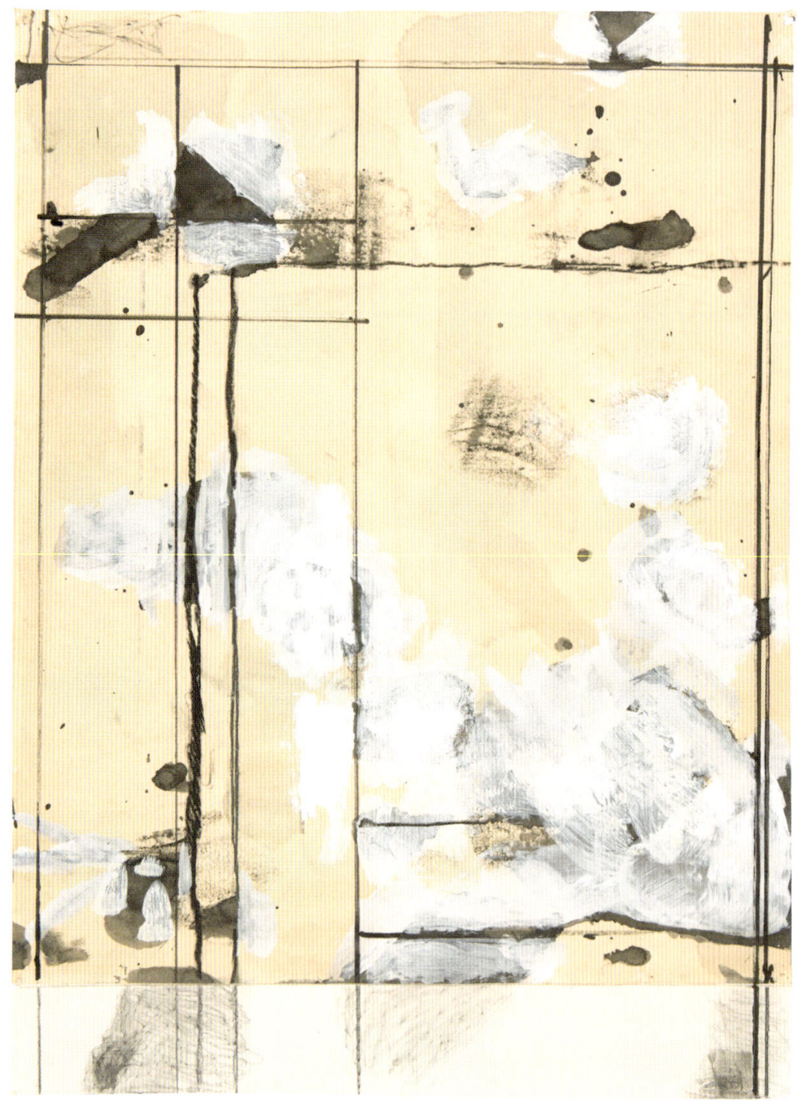

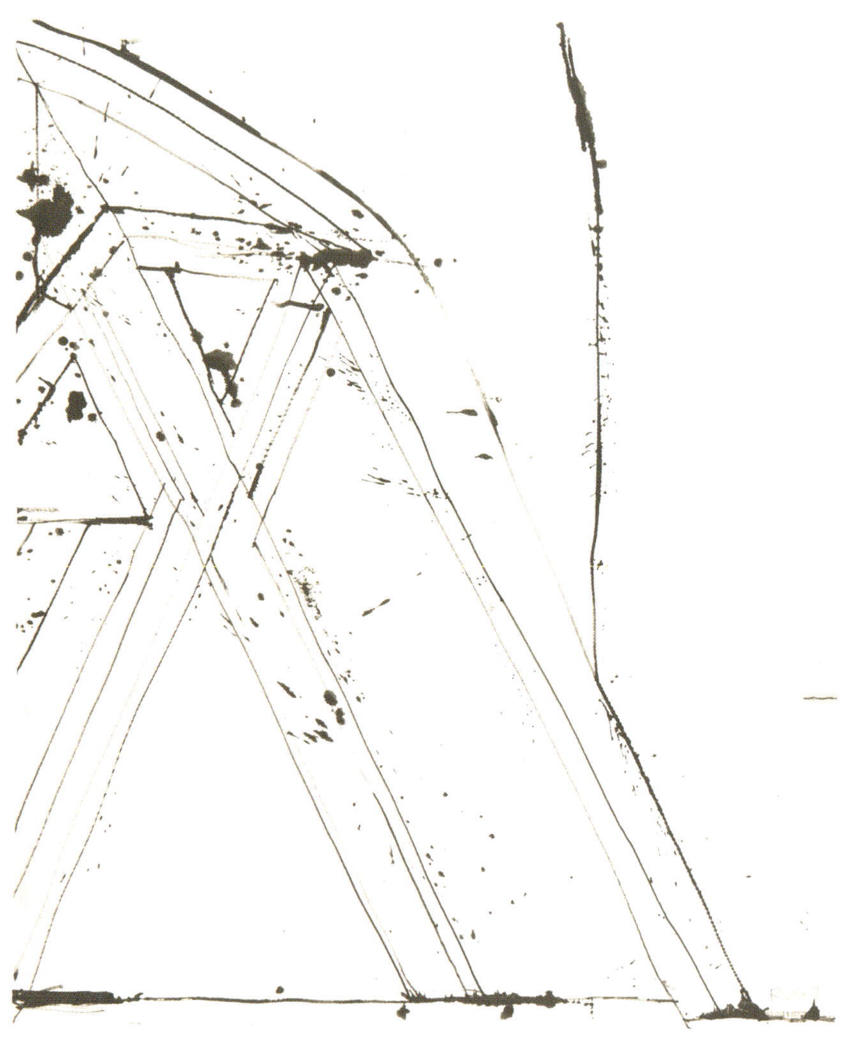

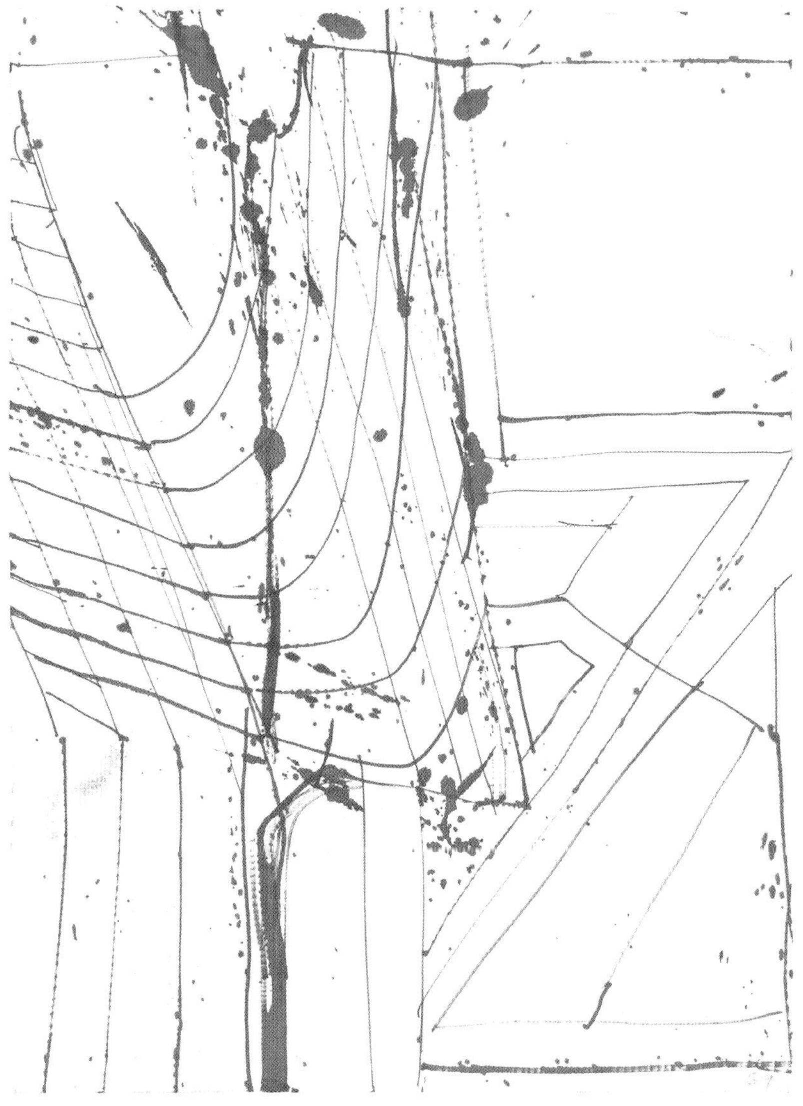

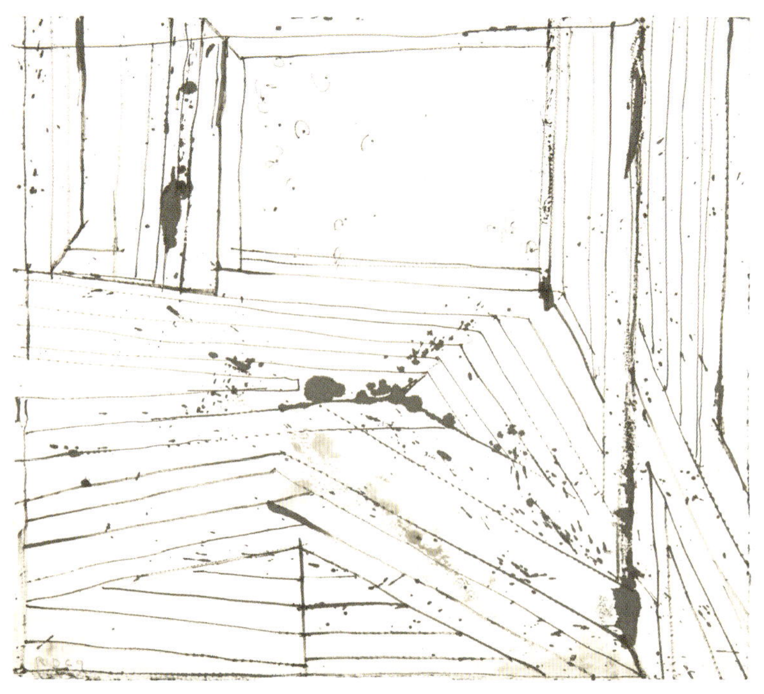

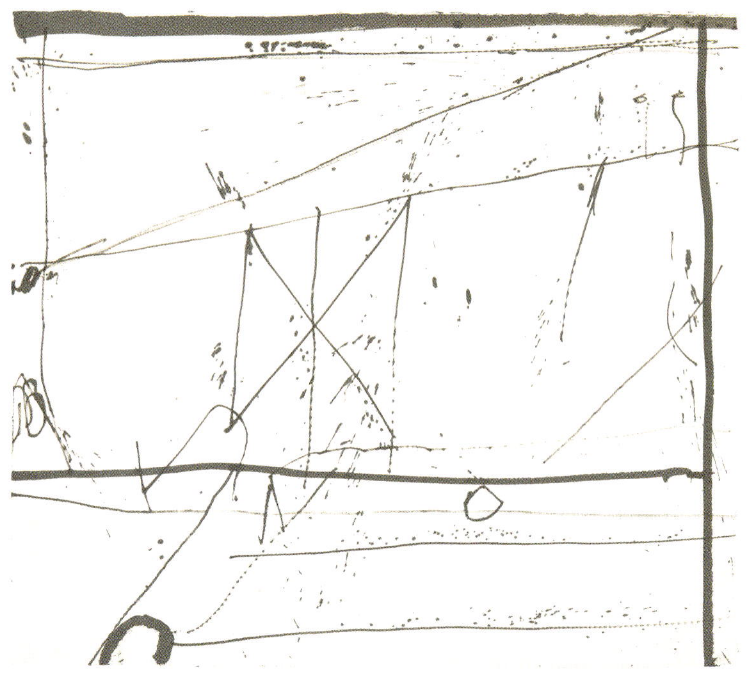

One wants to see the artifice of the thing as well as the subject.

· · · ·

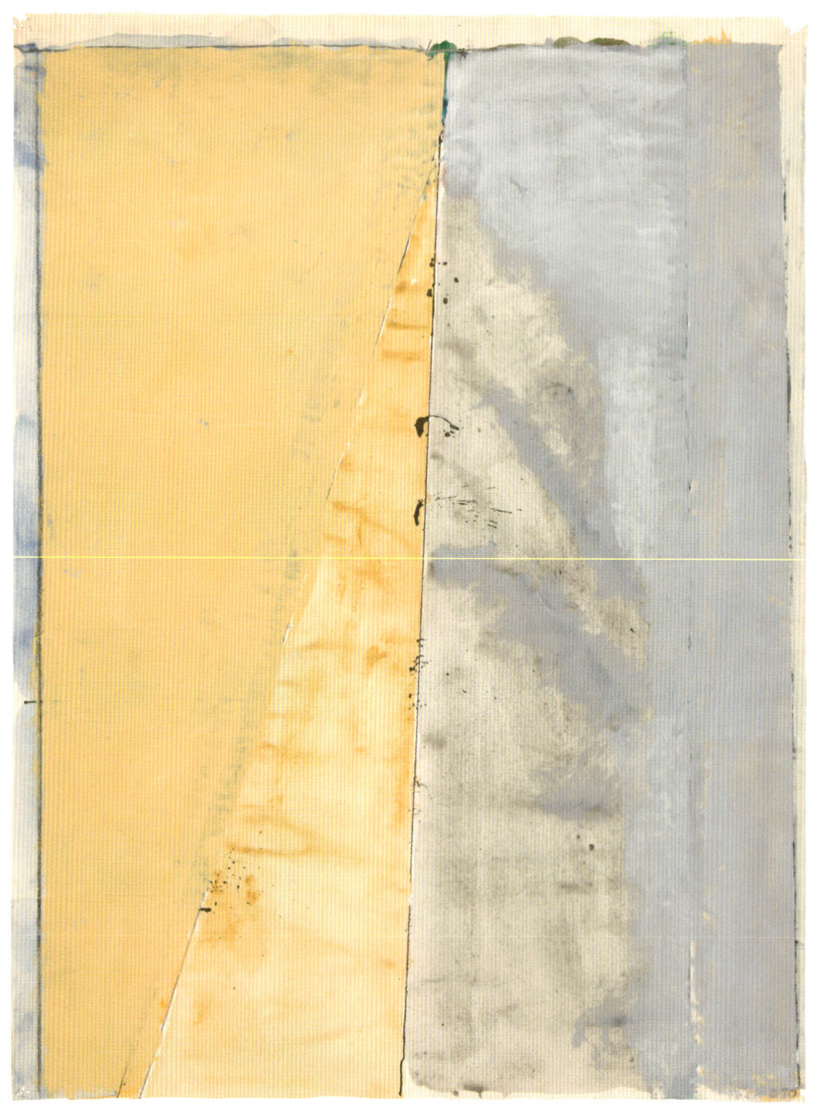

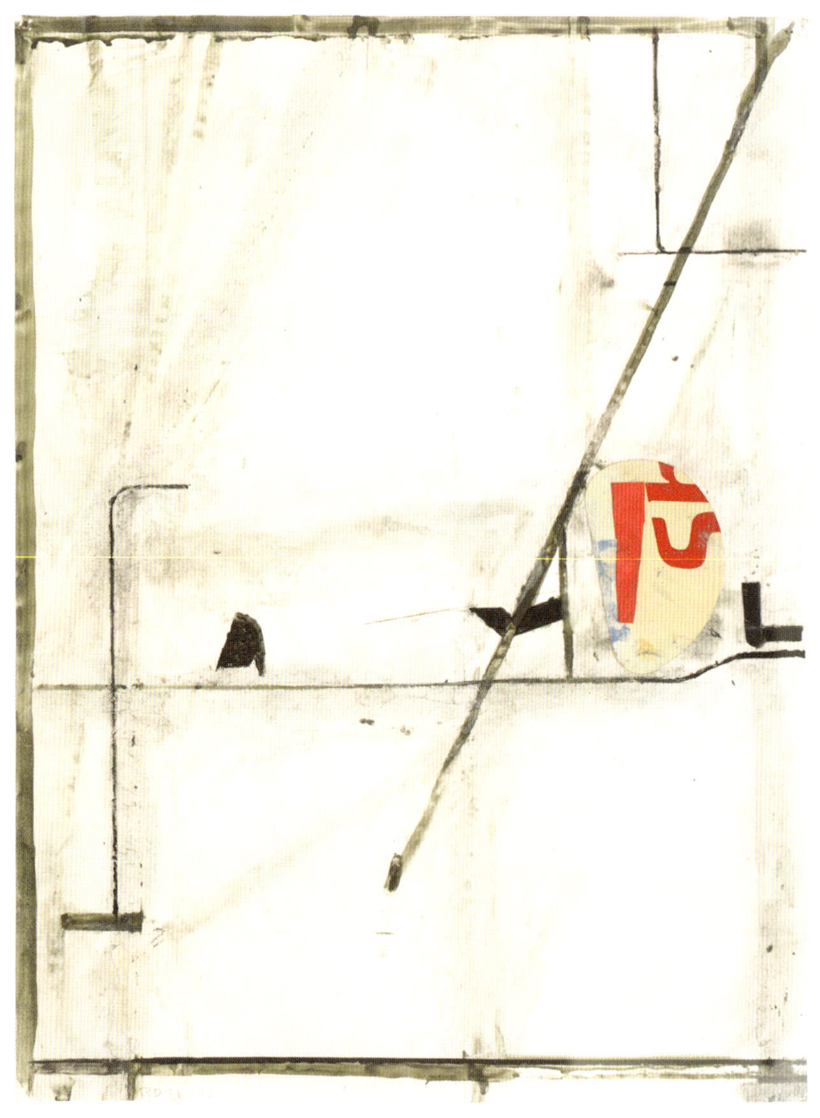

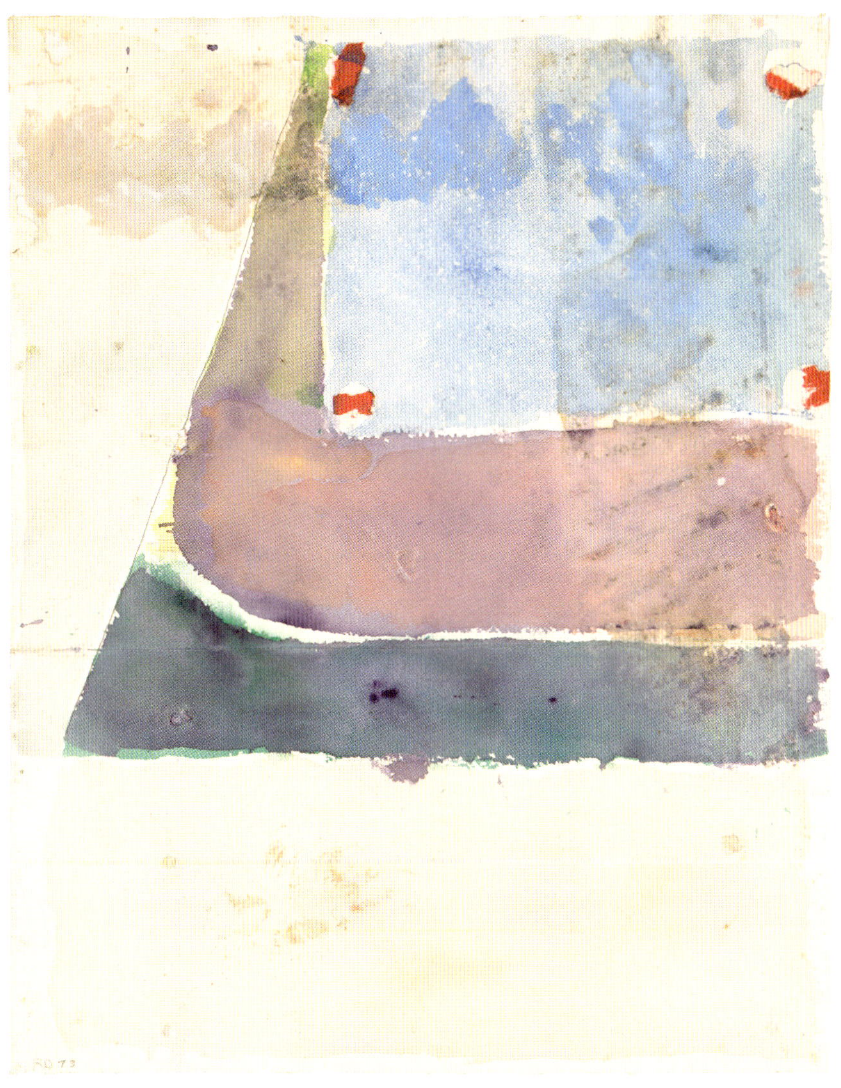

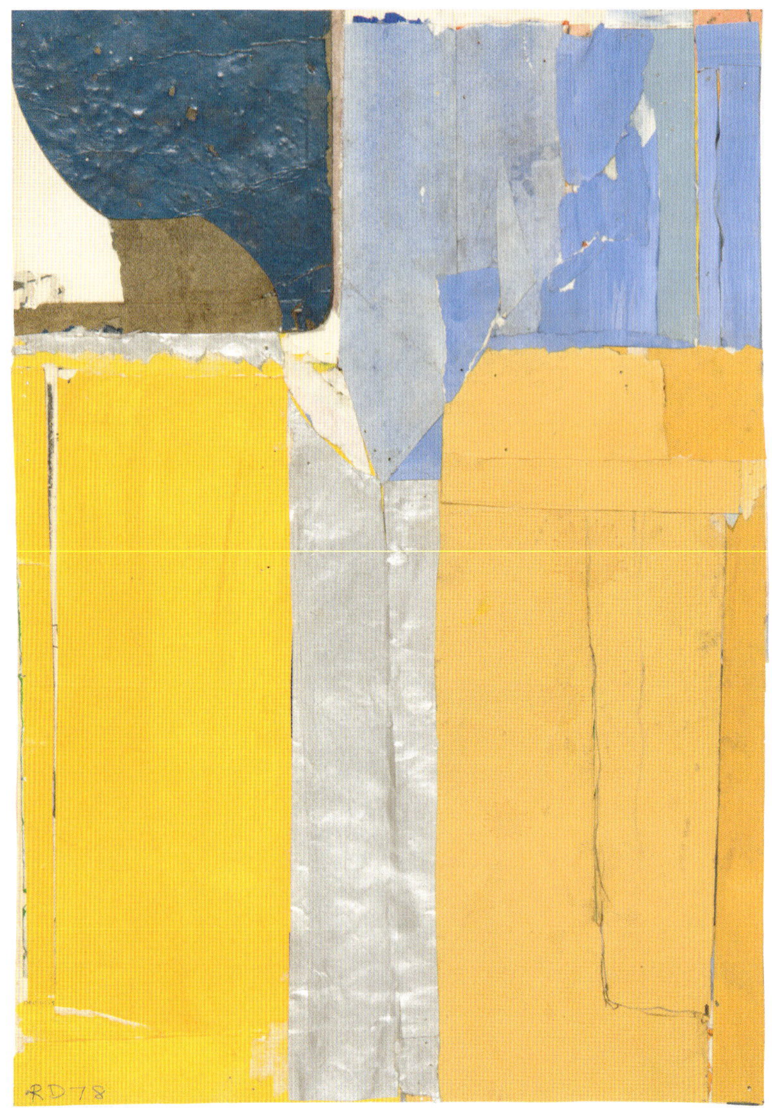
RD78

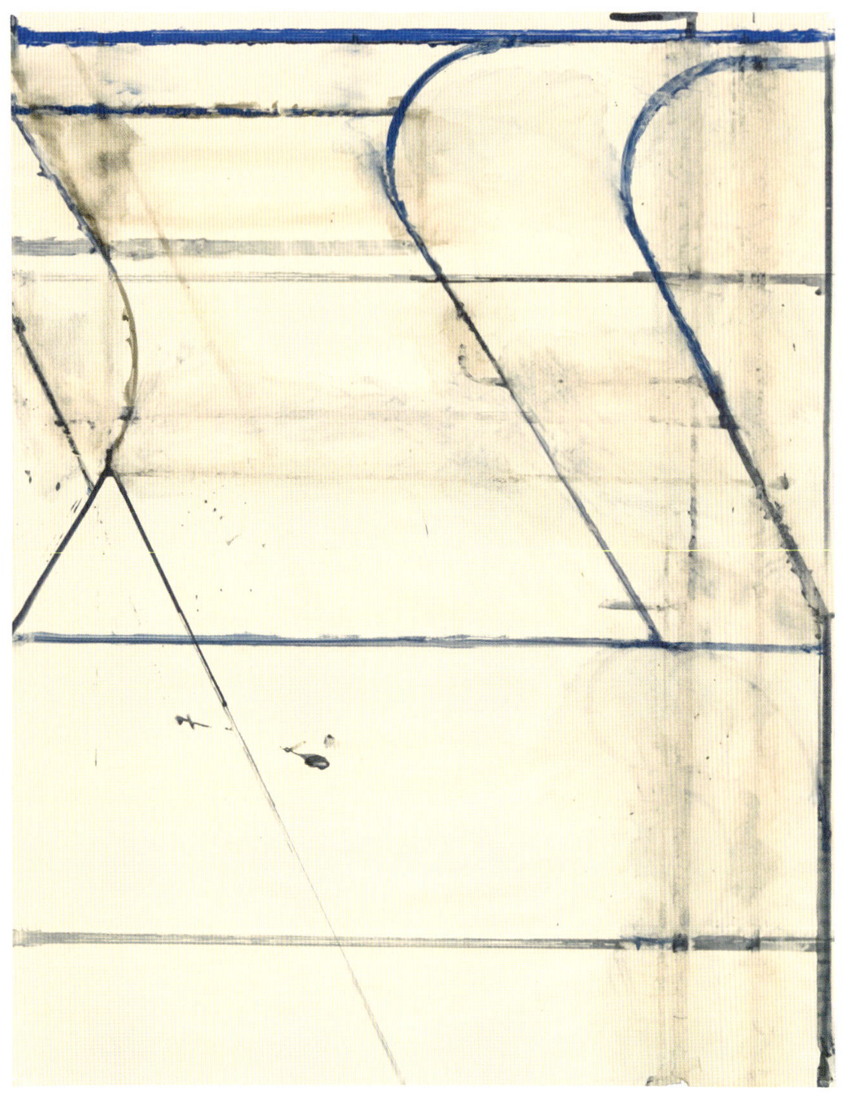

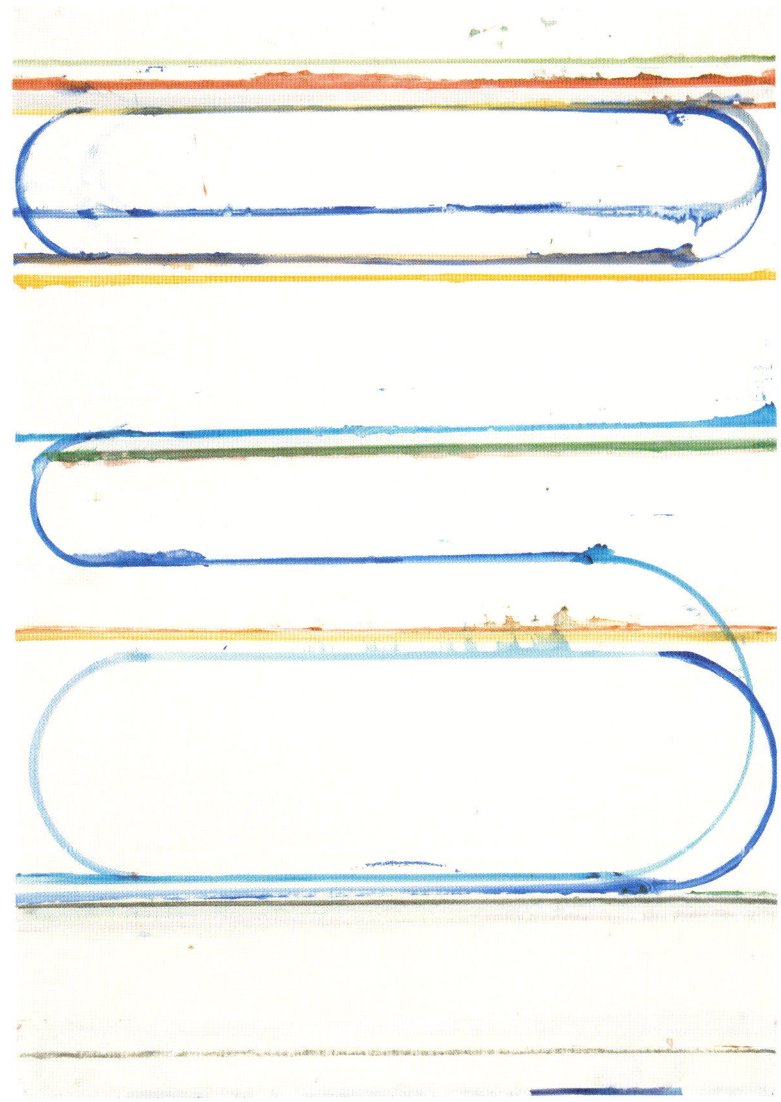

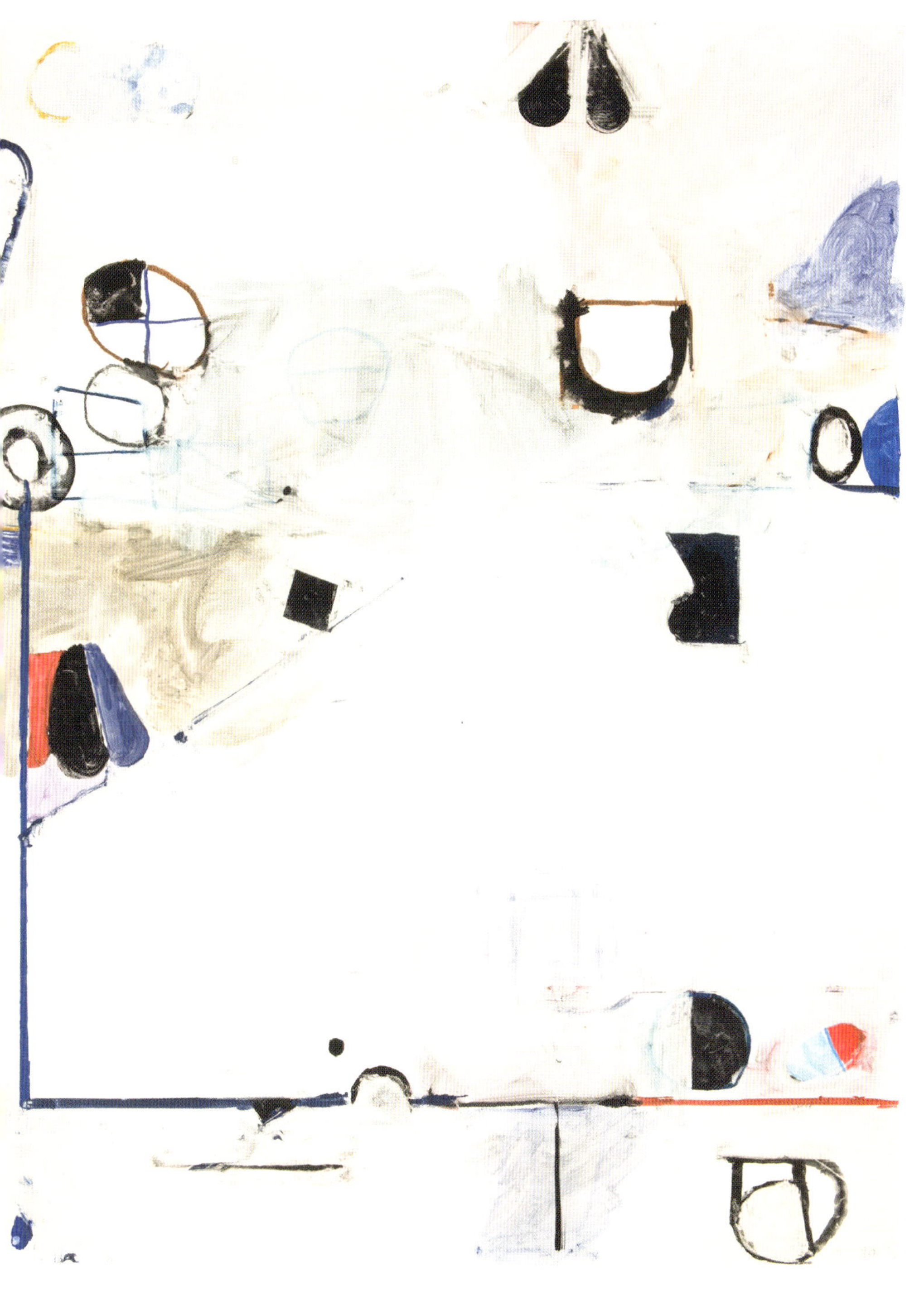

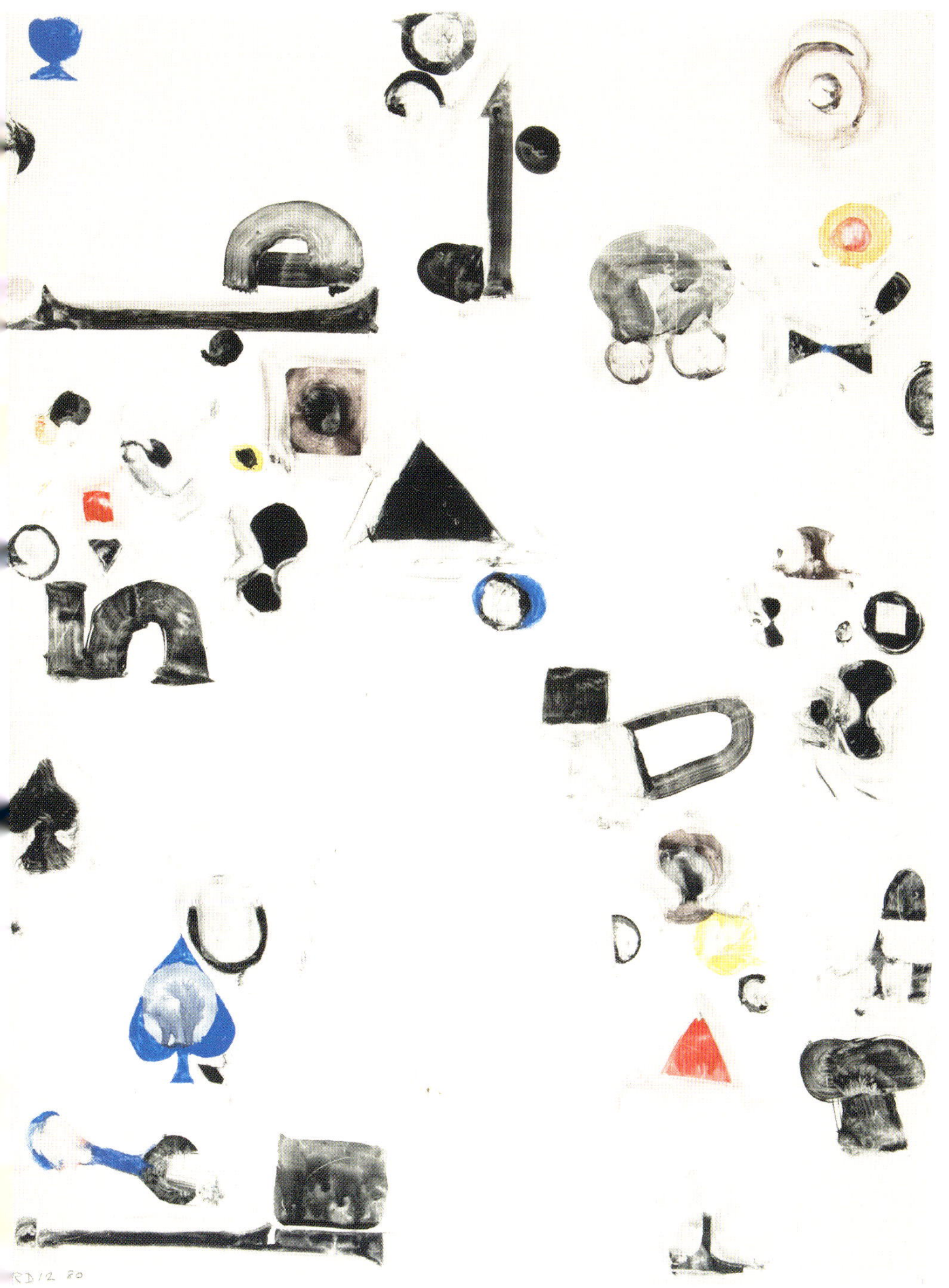
RD12 80

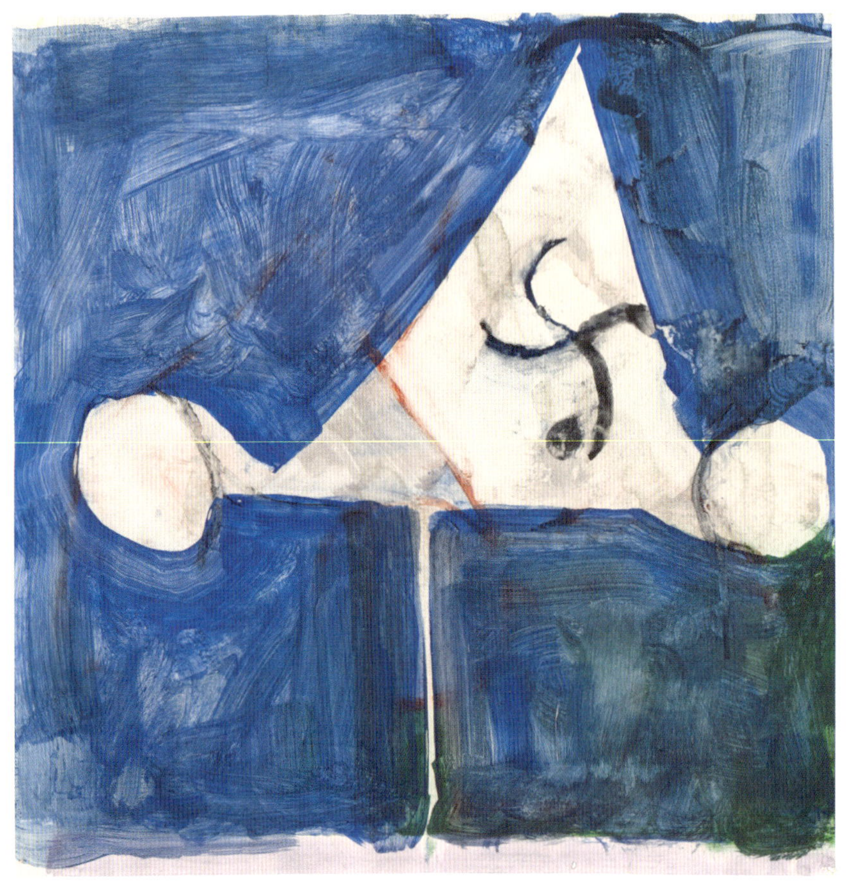

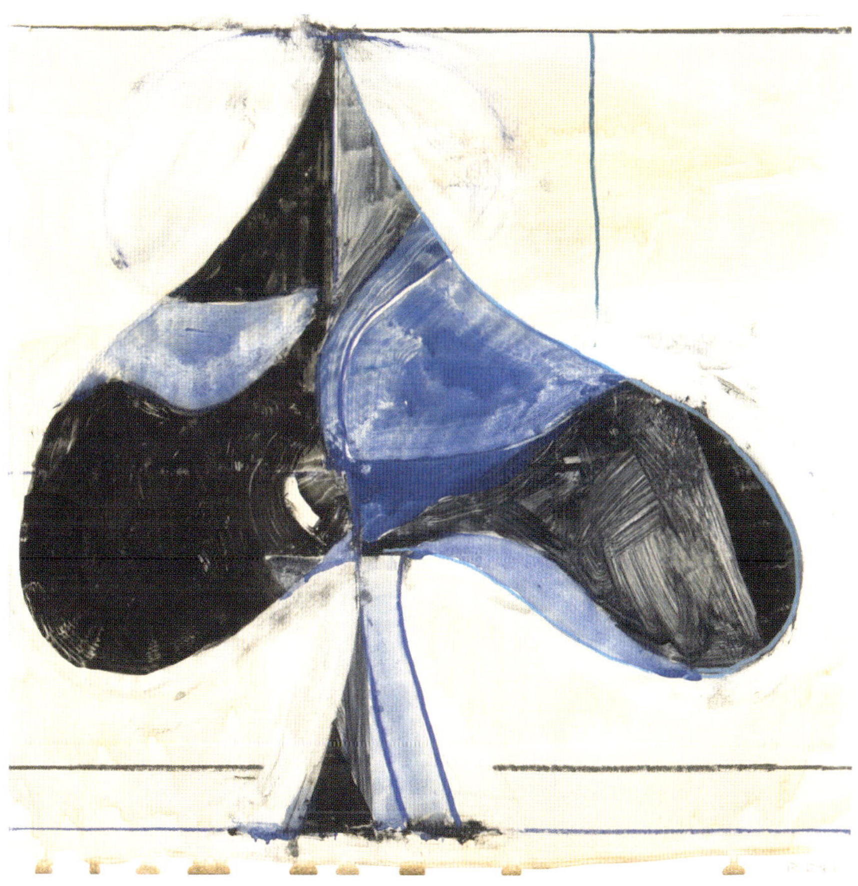

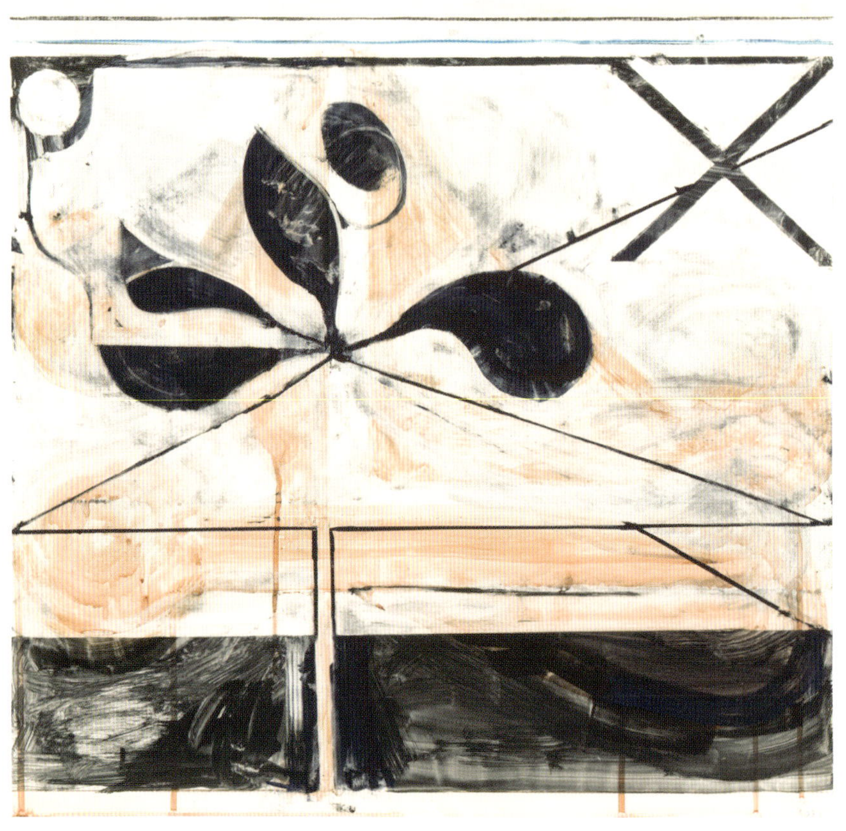

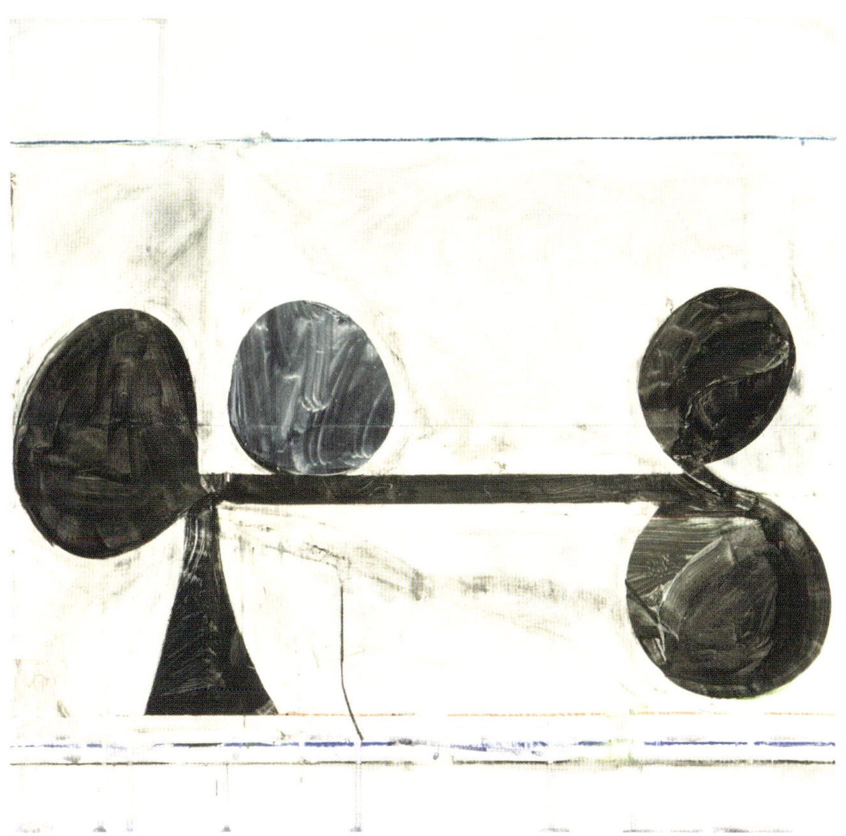

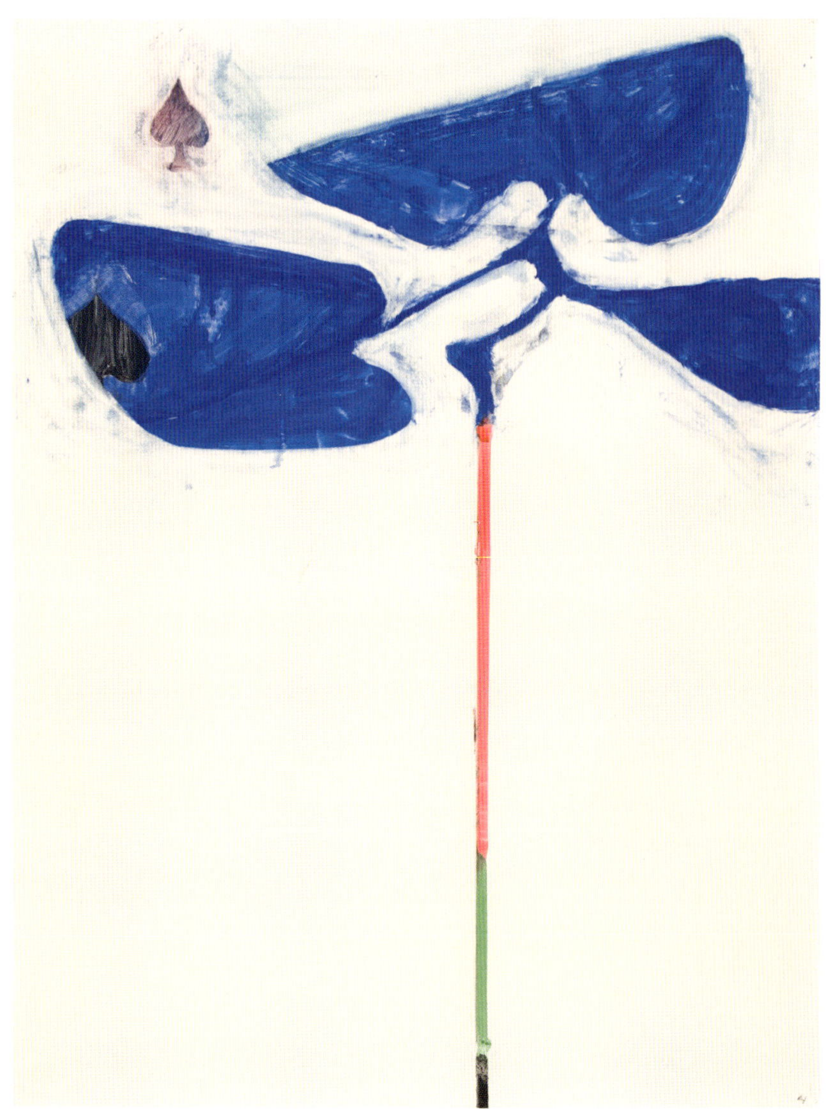

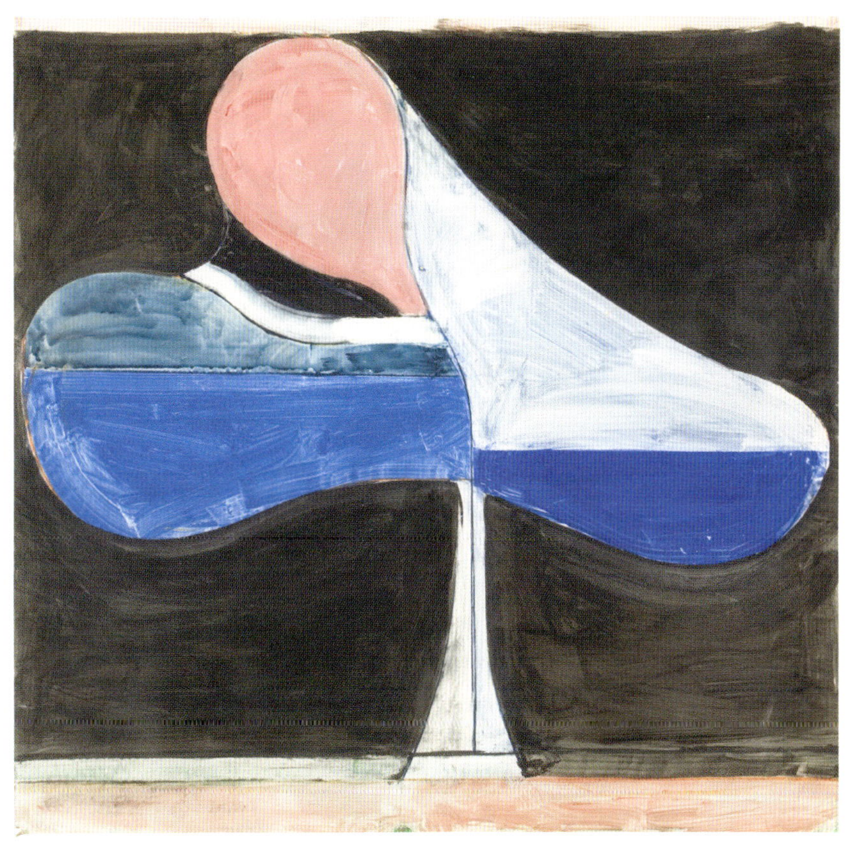

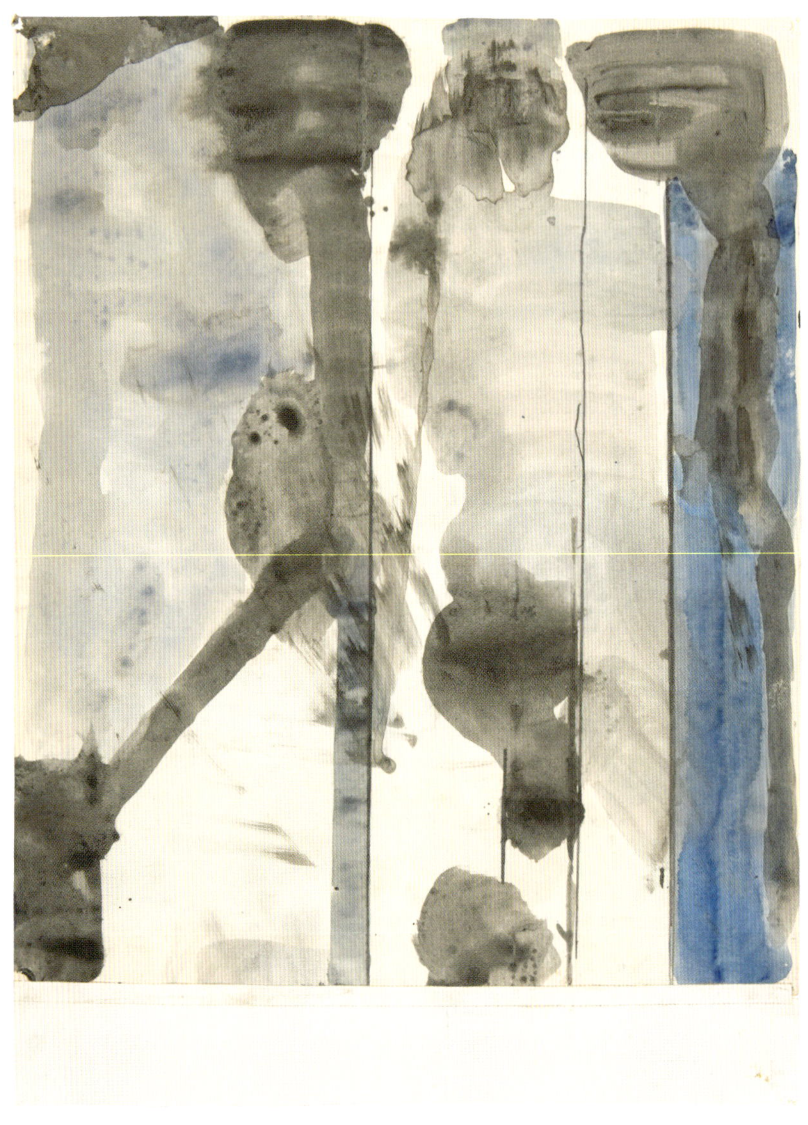

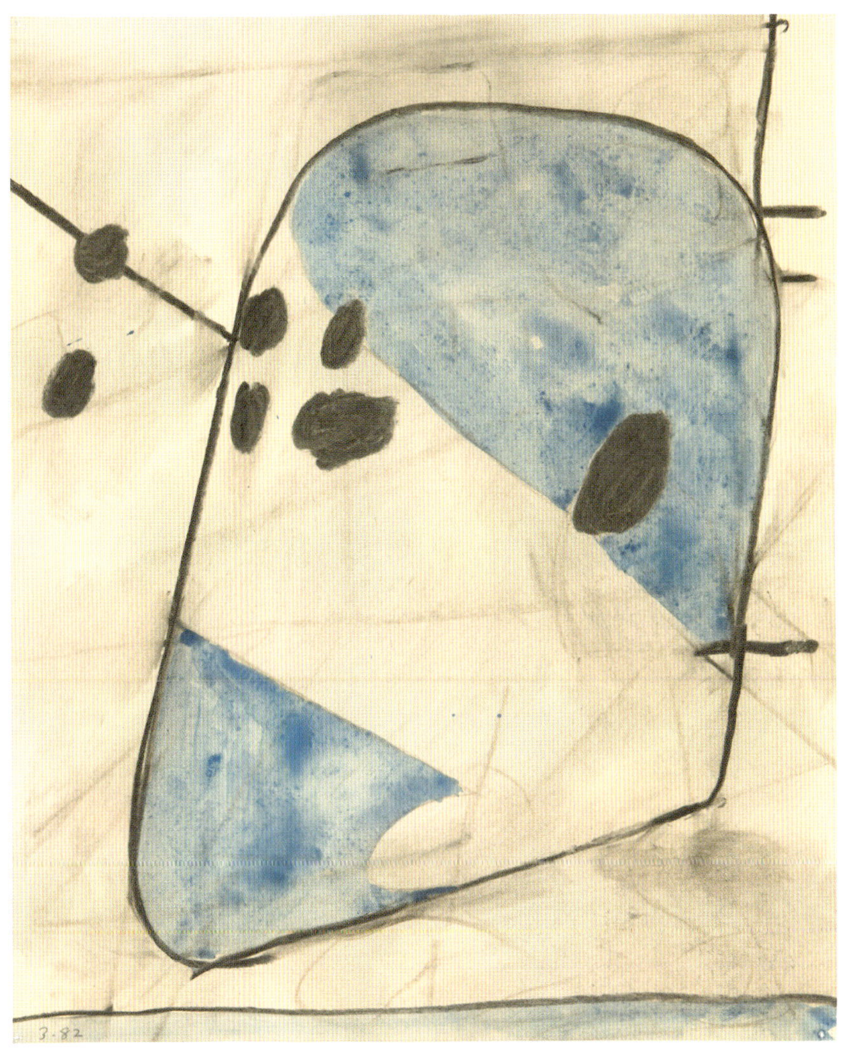
3-82

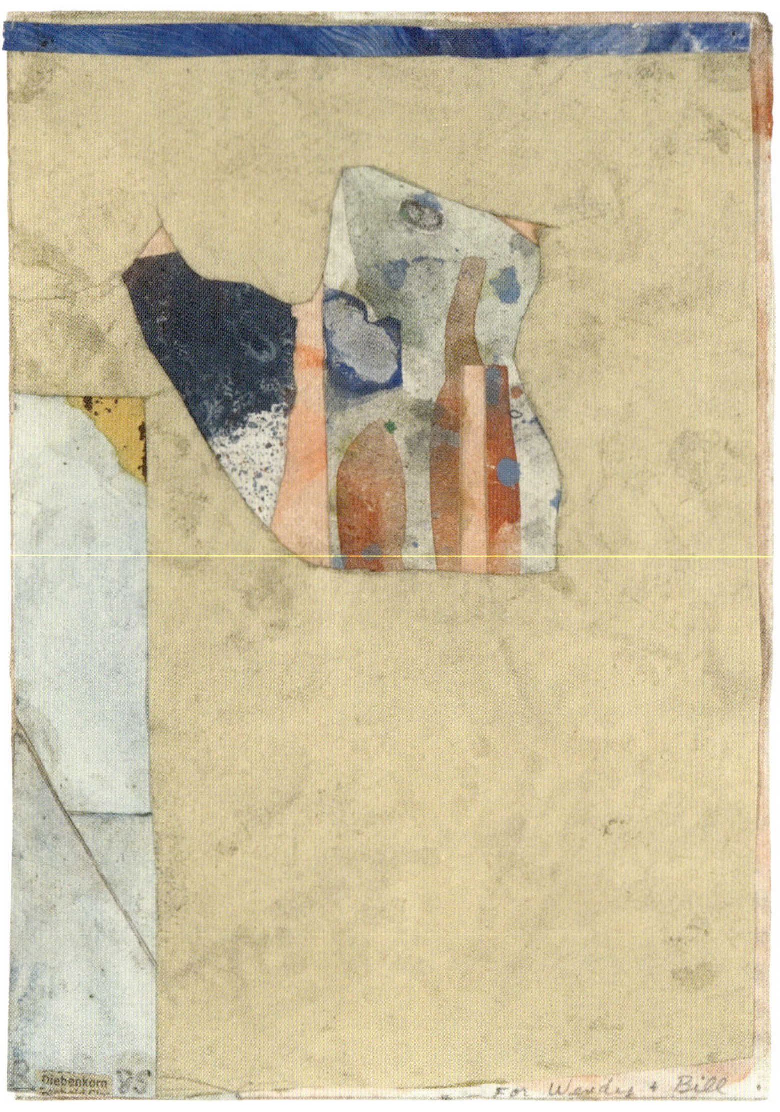
Diebenkorn
85
For Wendy + Bill

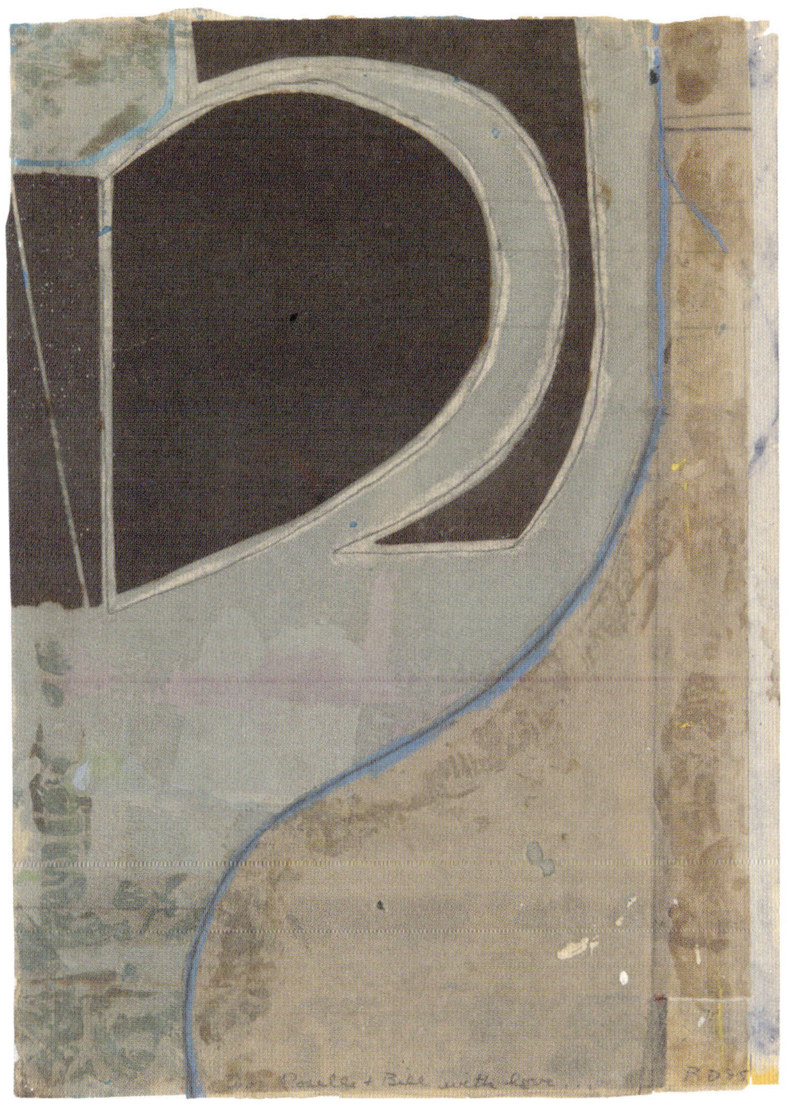

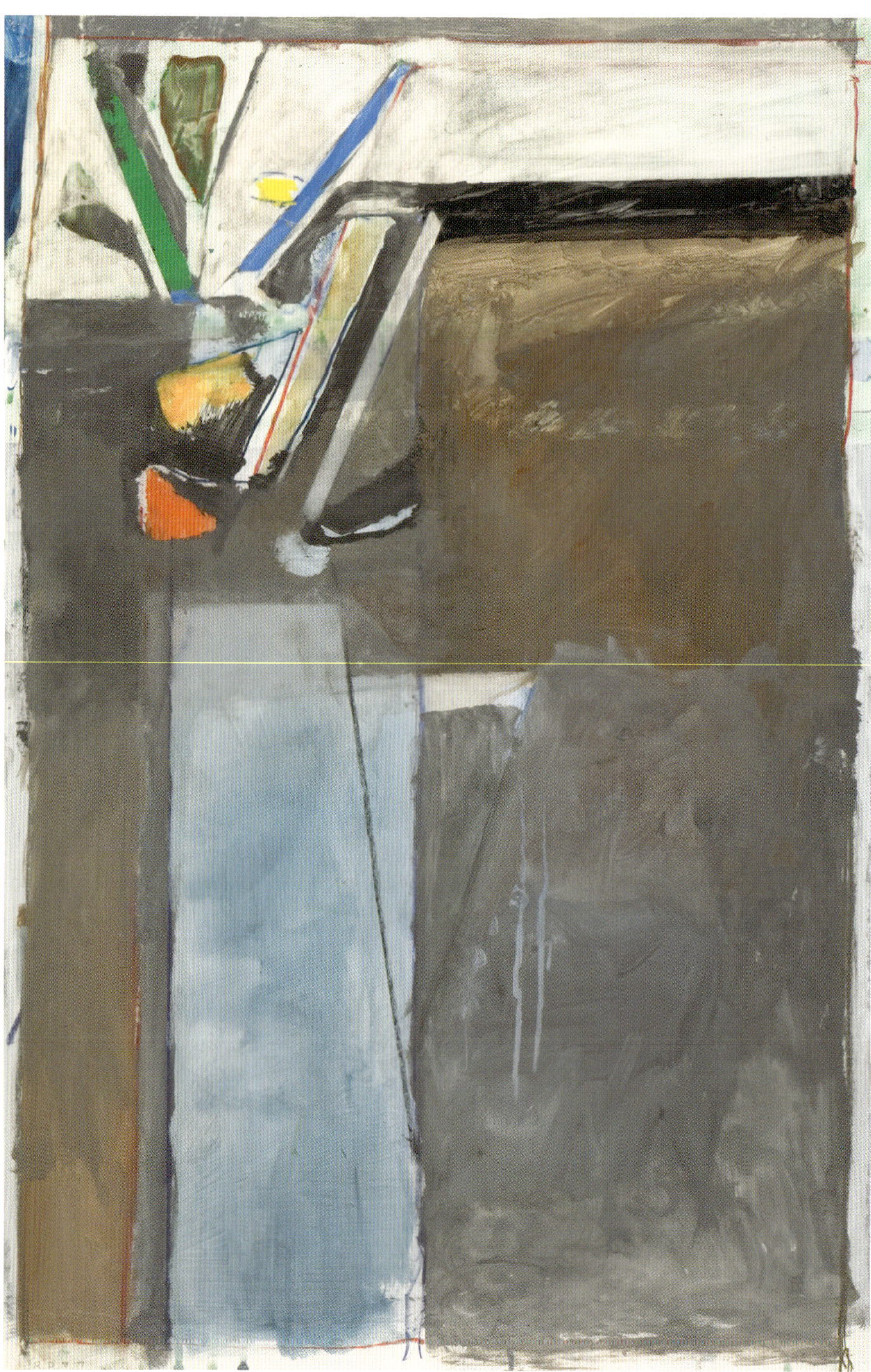

I'm not comfortable being, altogether comfortable, being accepted.

· · · ·

HEALDSBURG

1988–1992

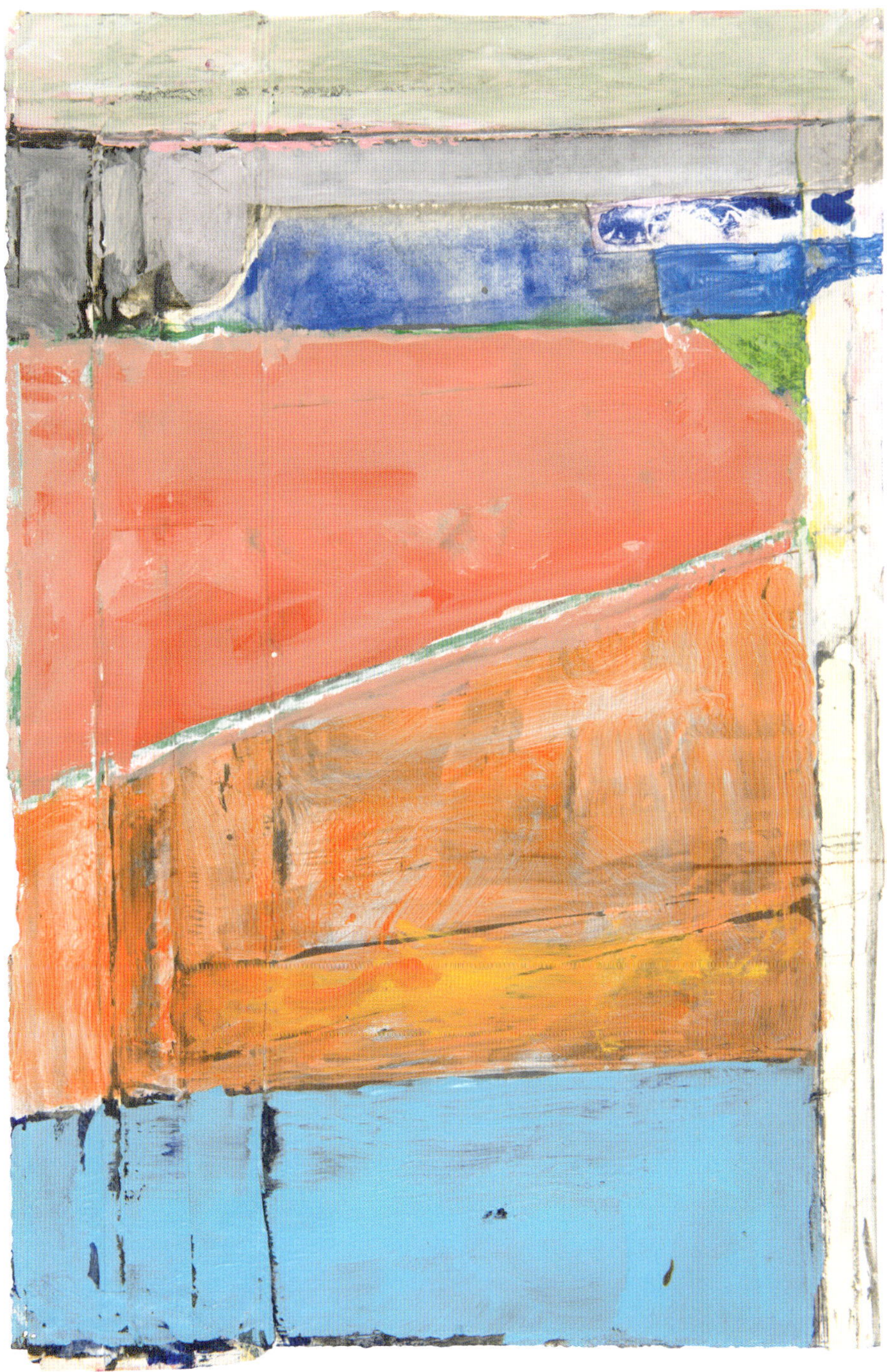

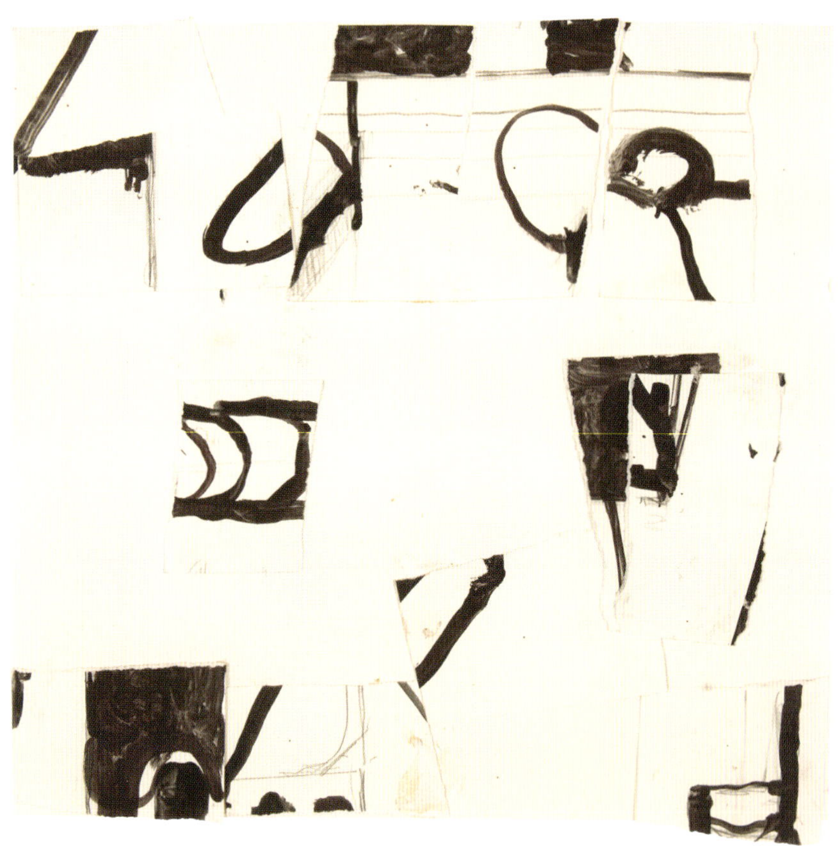

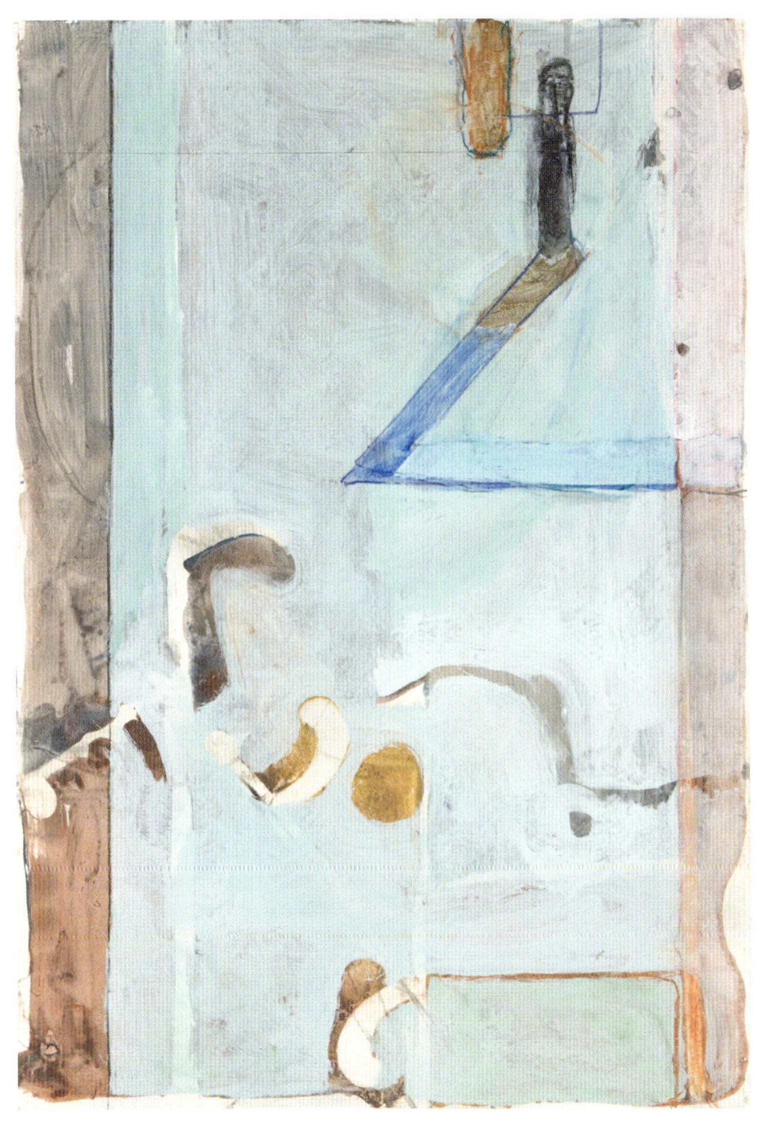

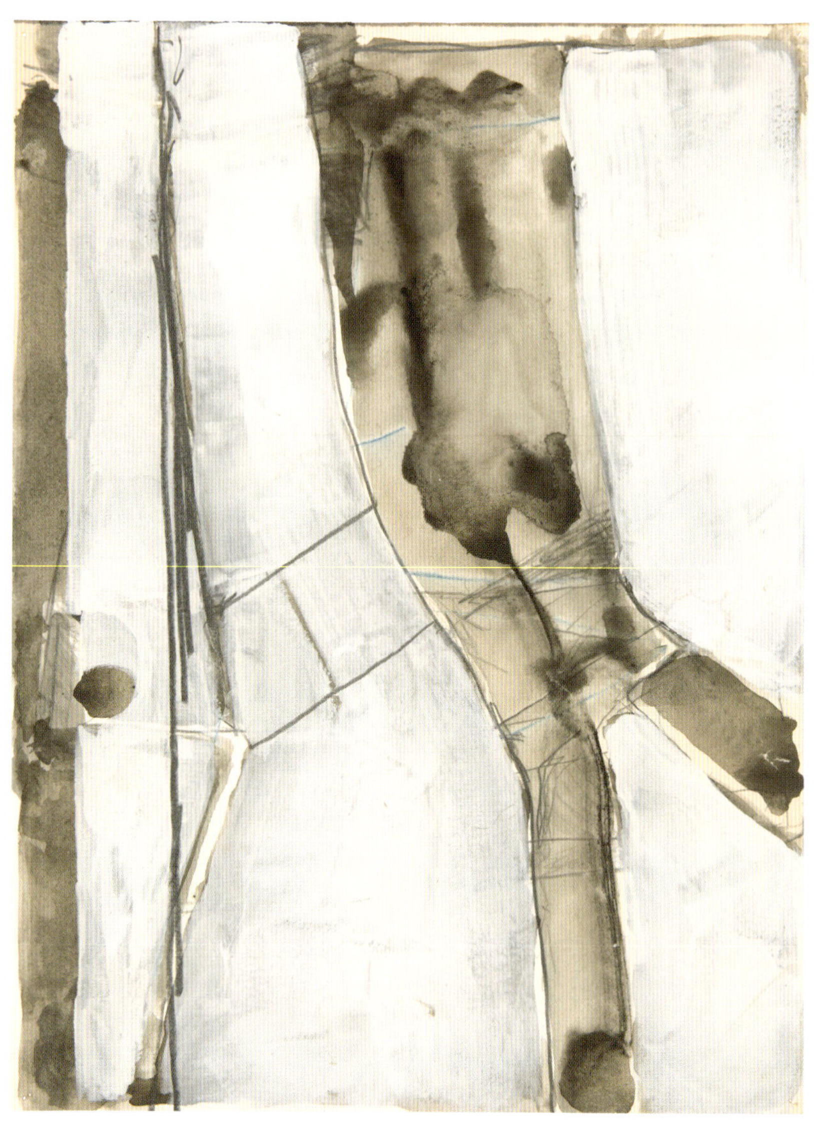

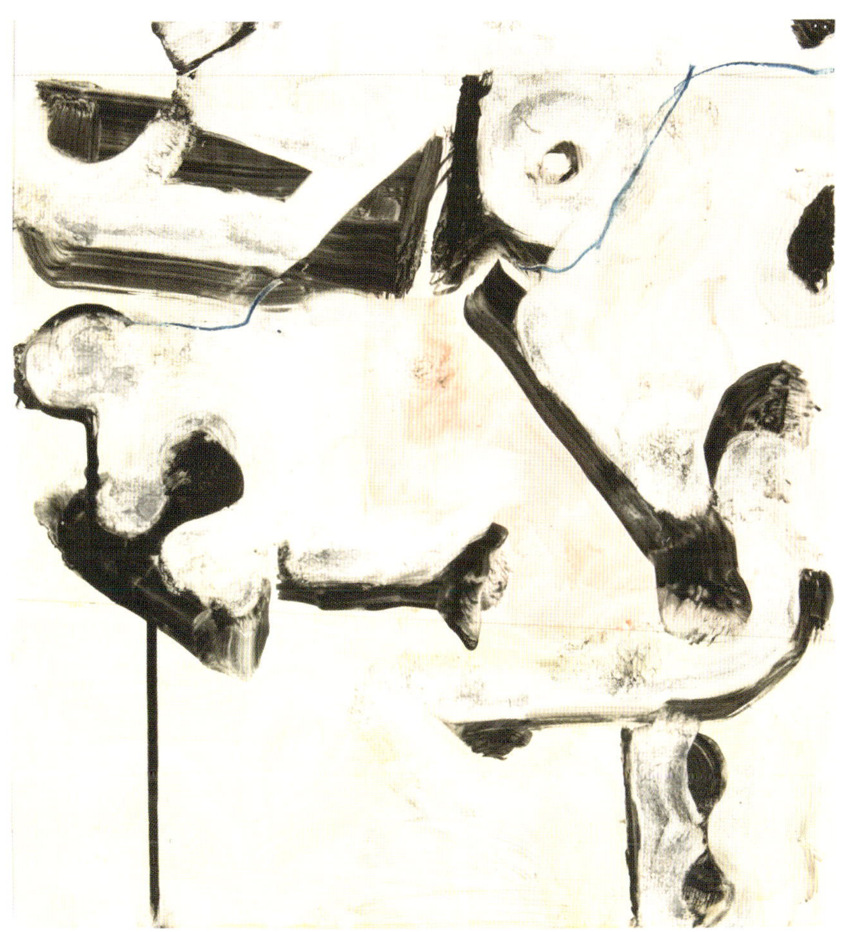

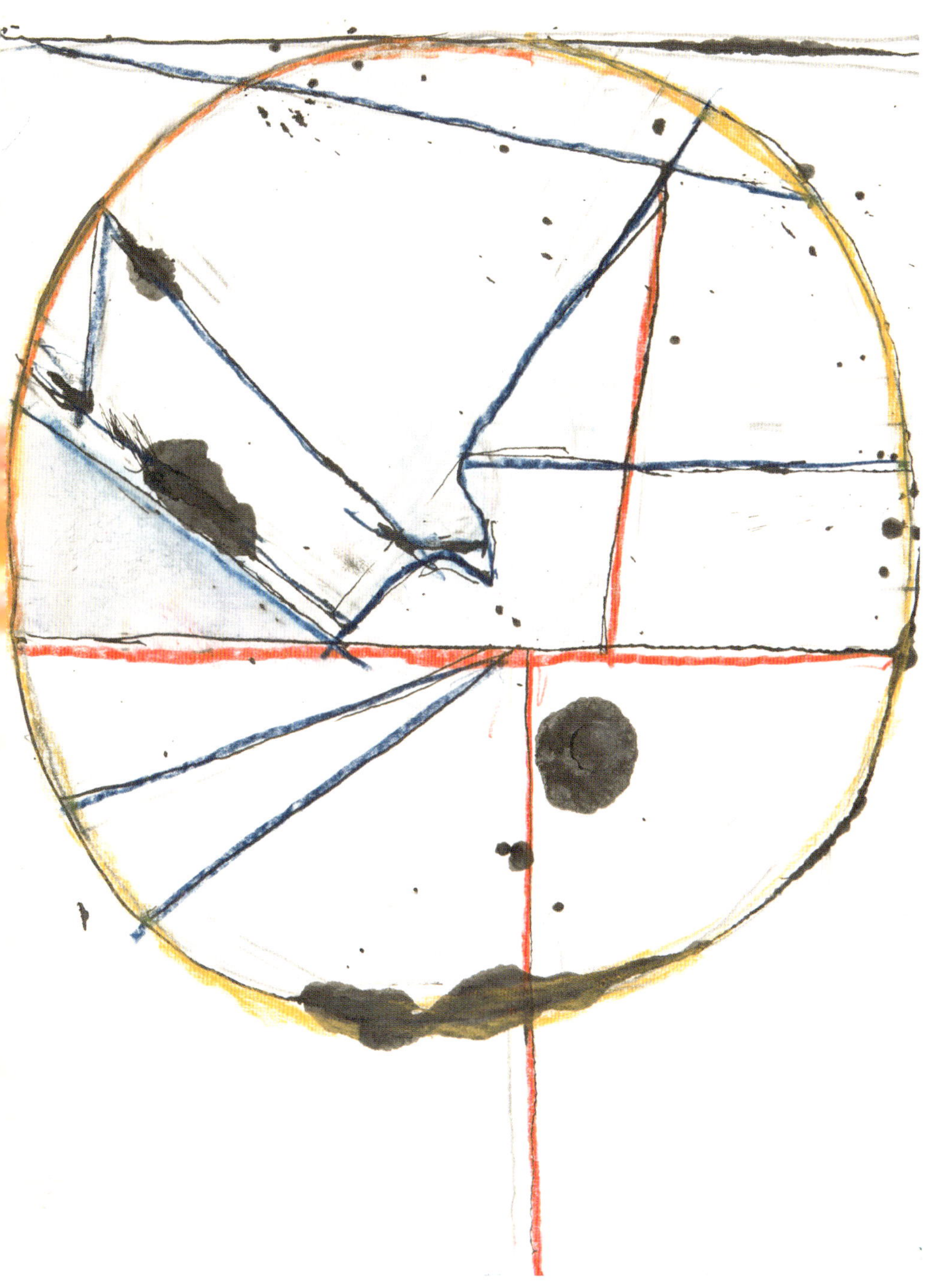

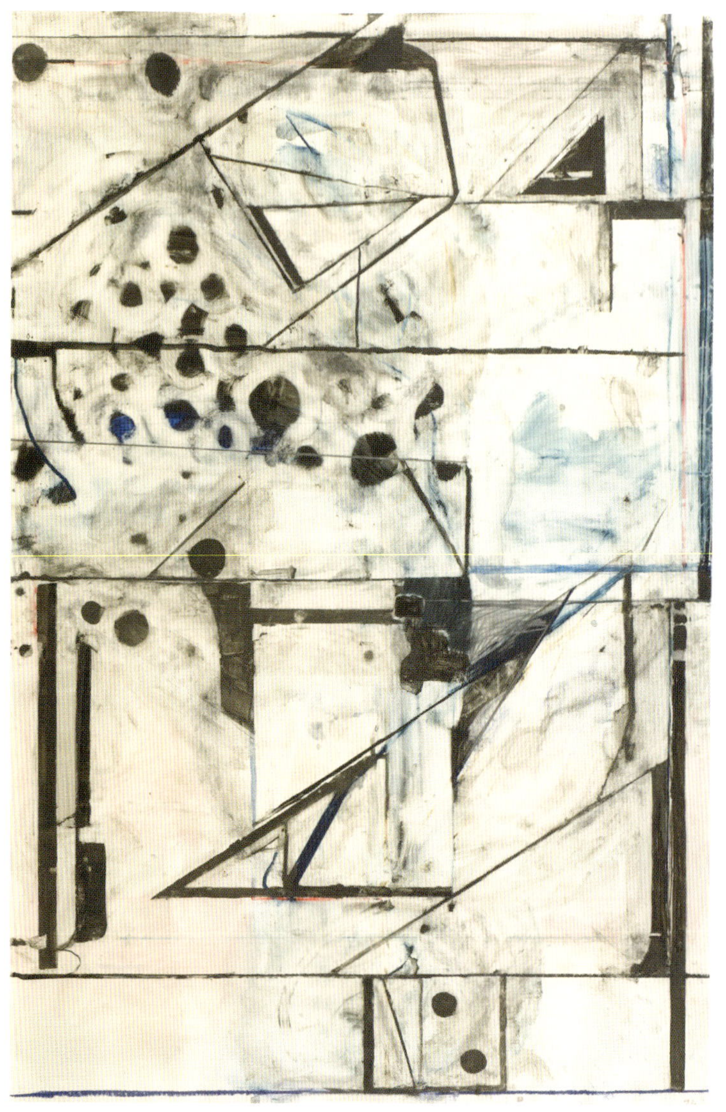

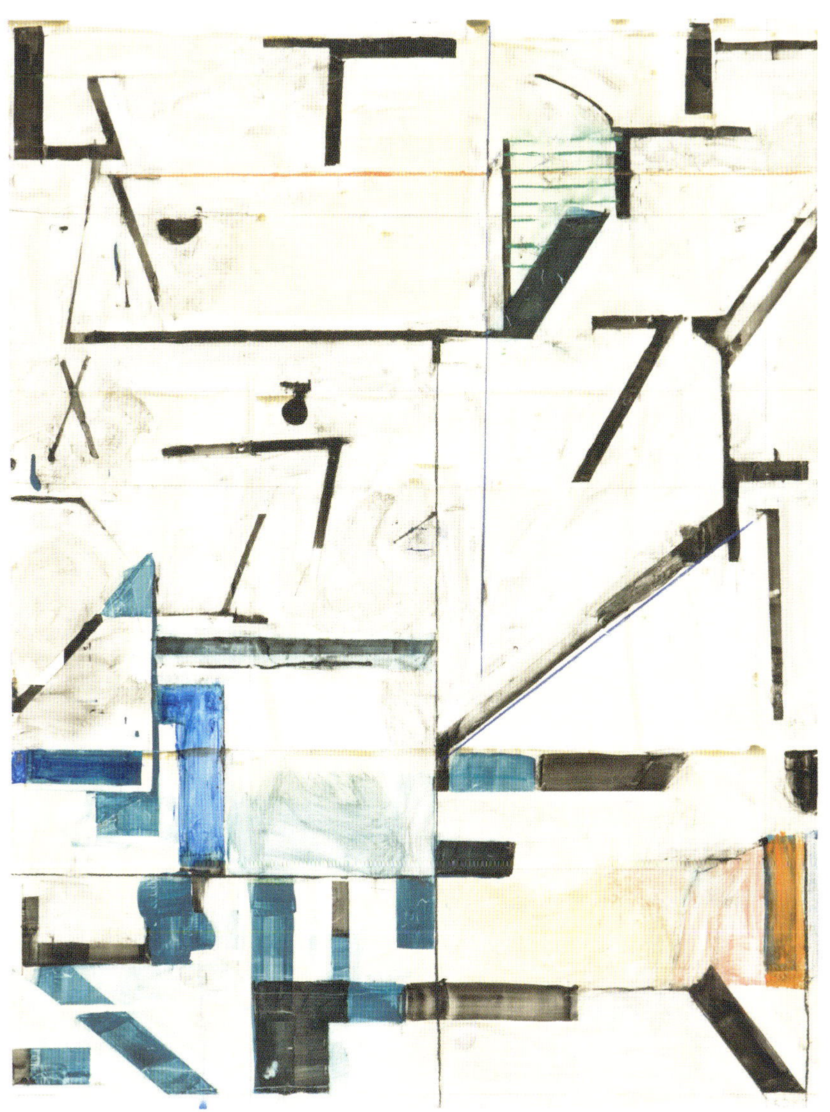

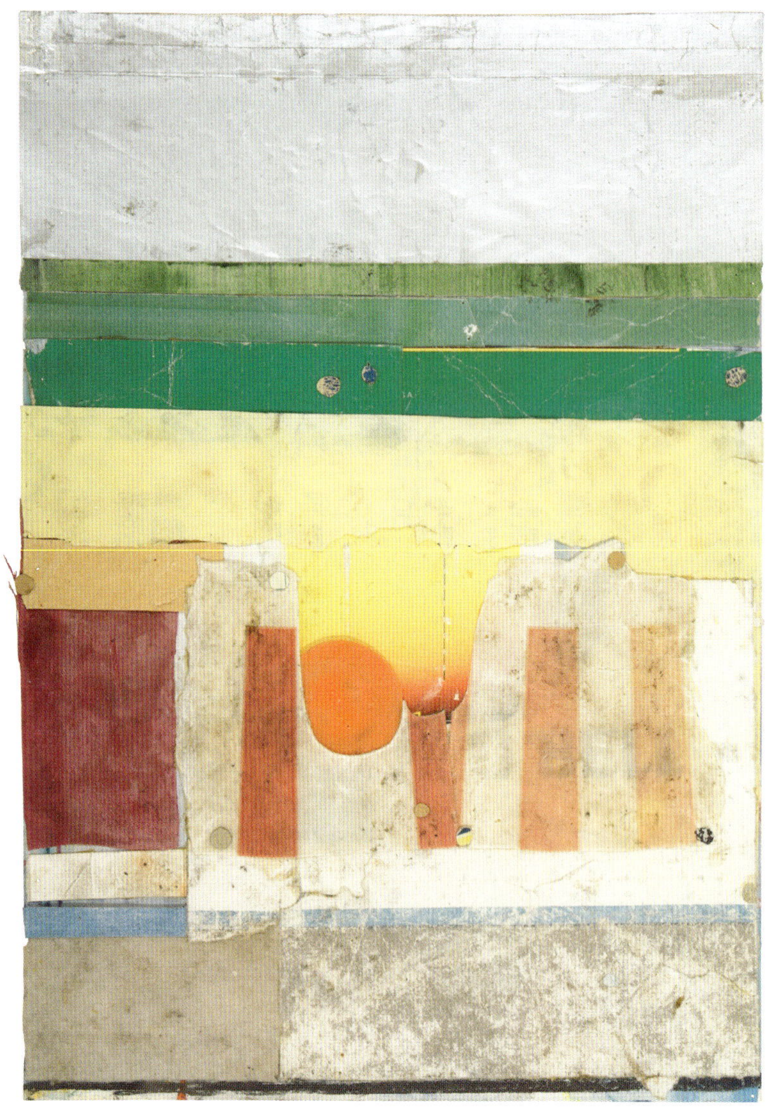

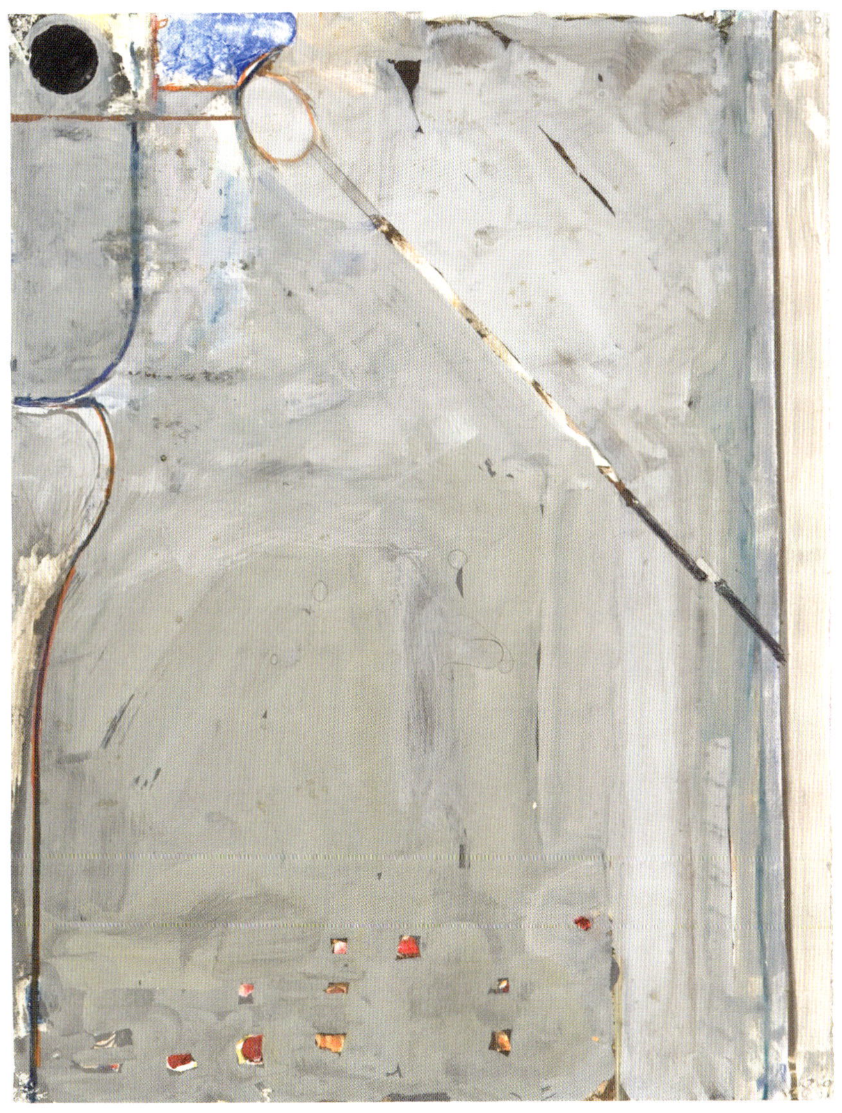

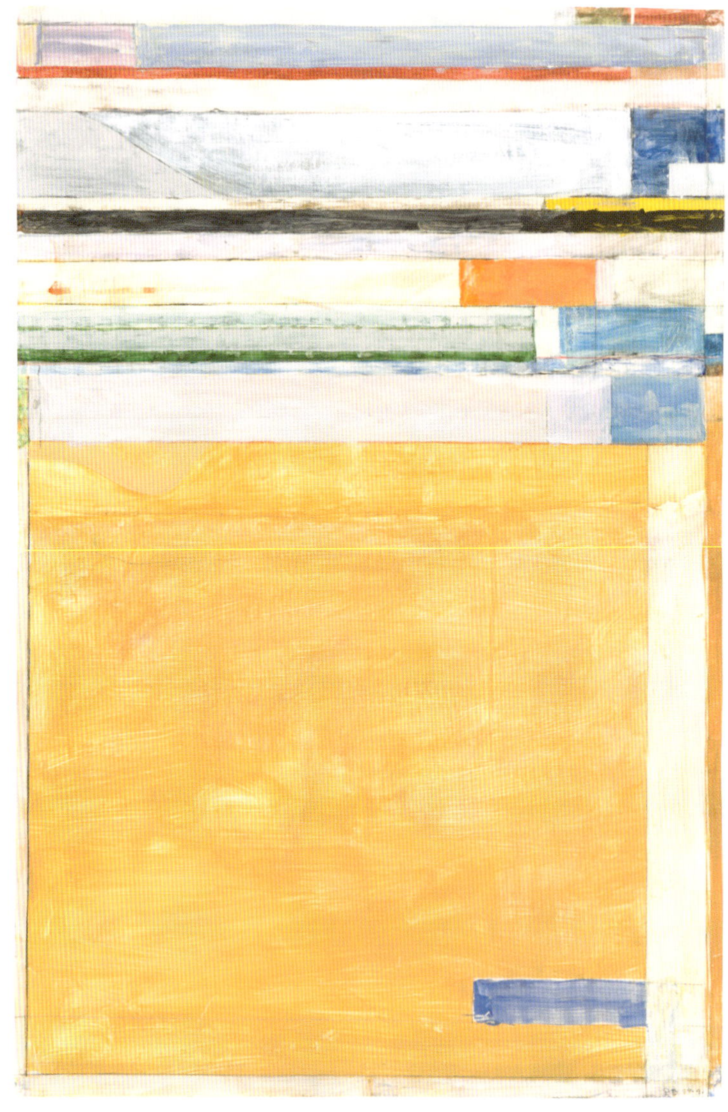

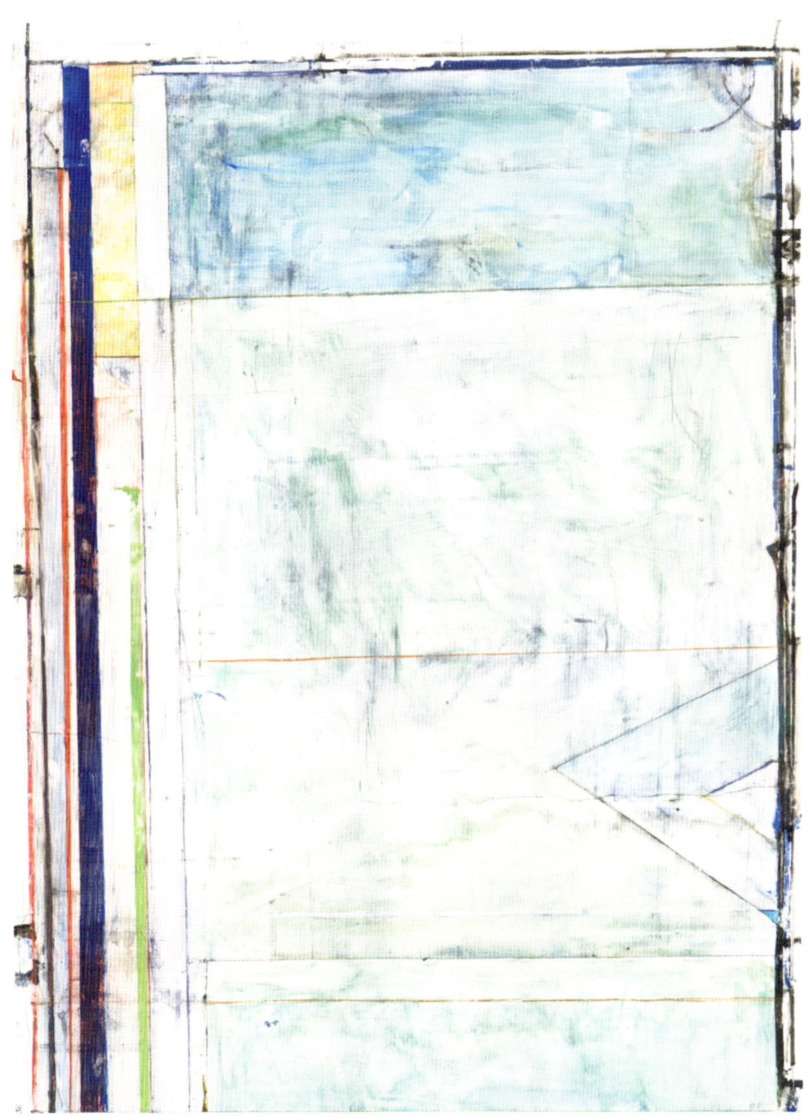

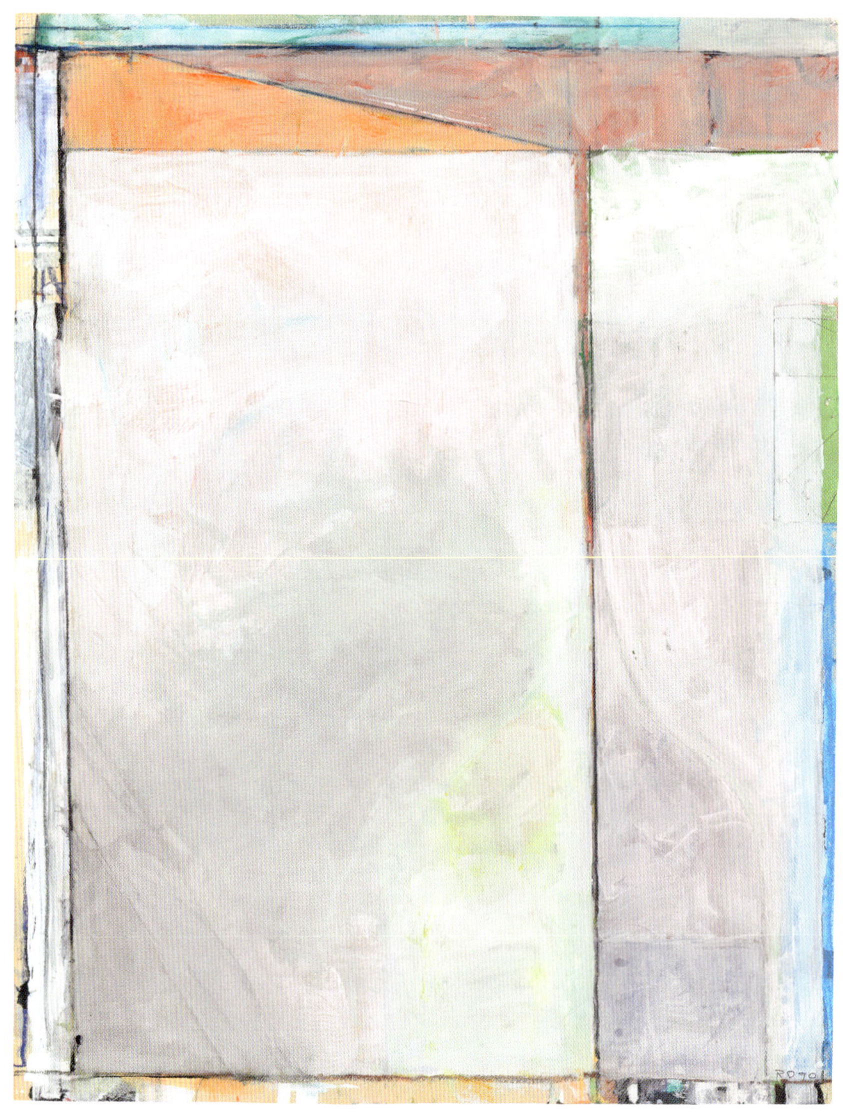

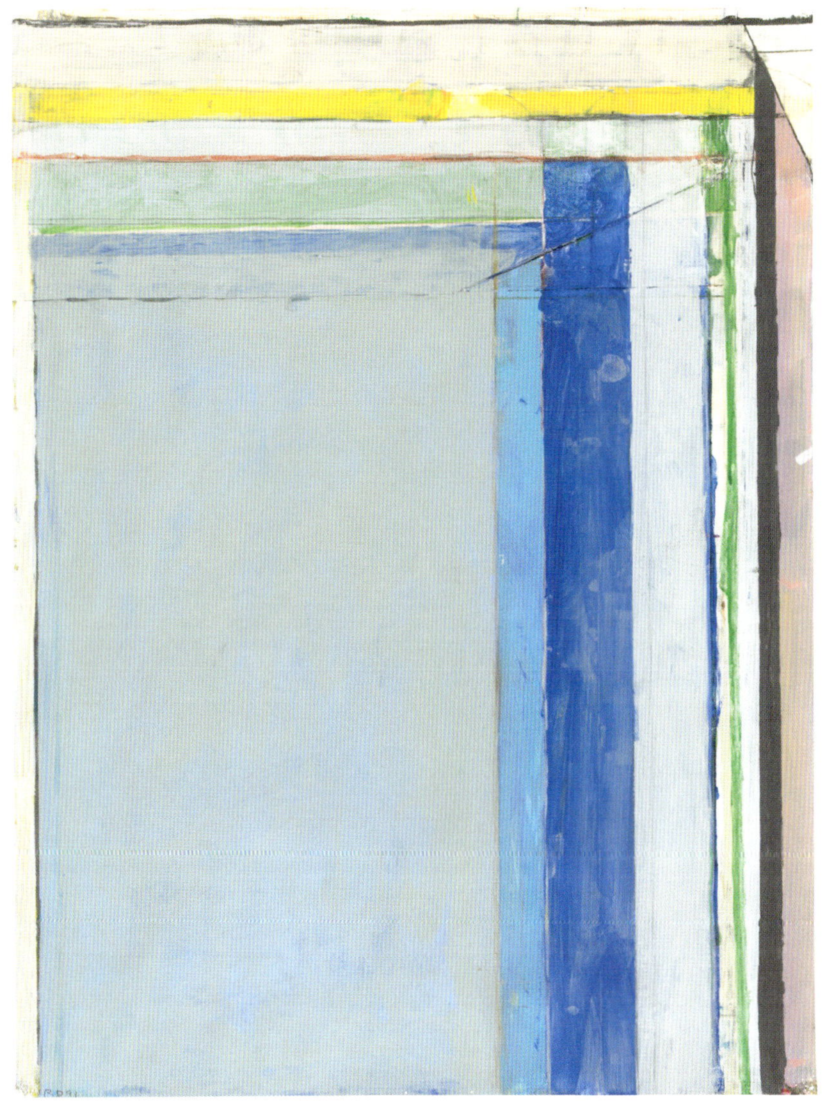

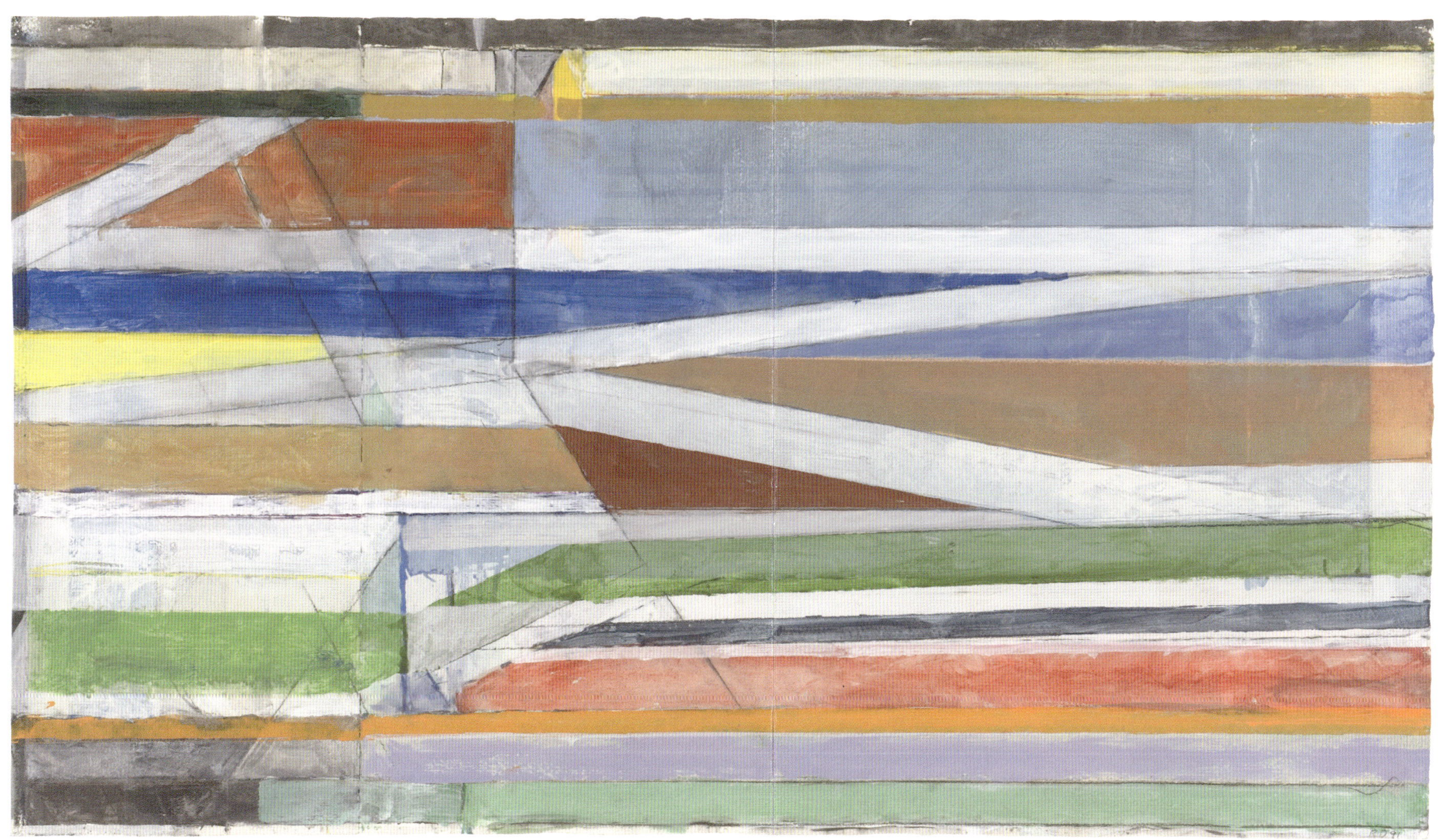

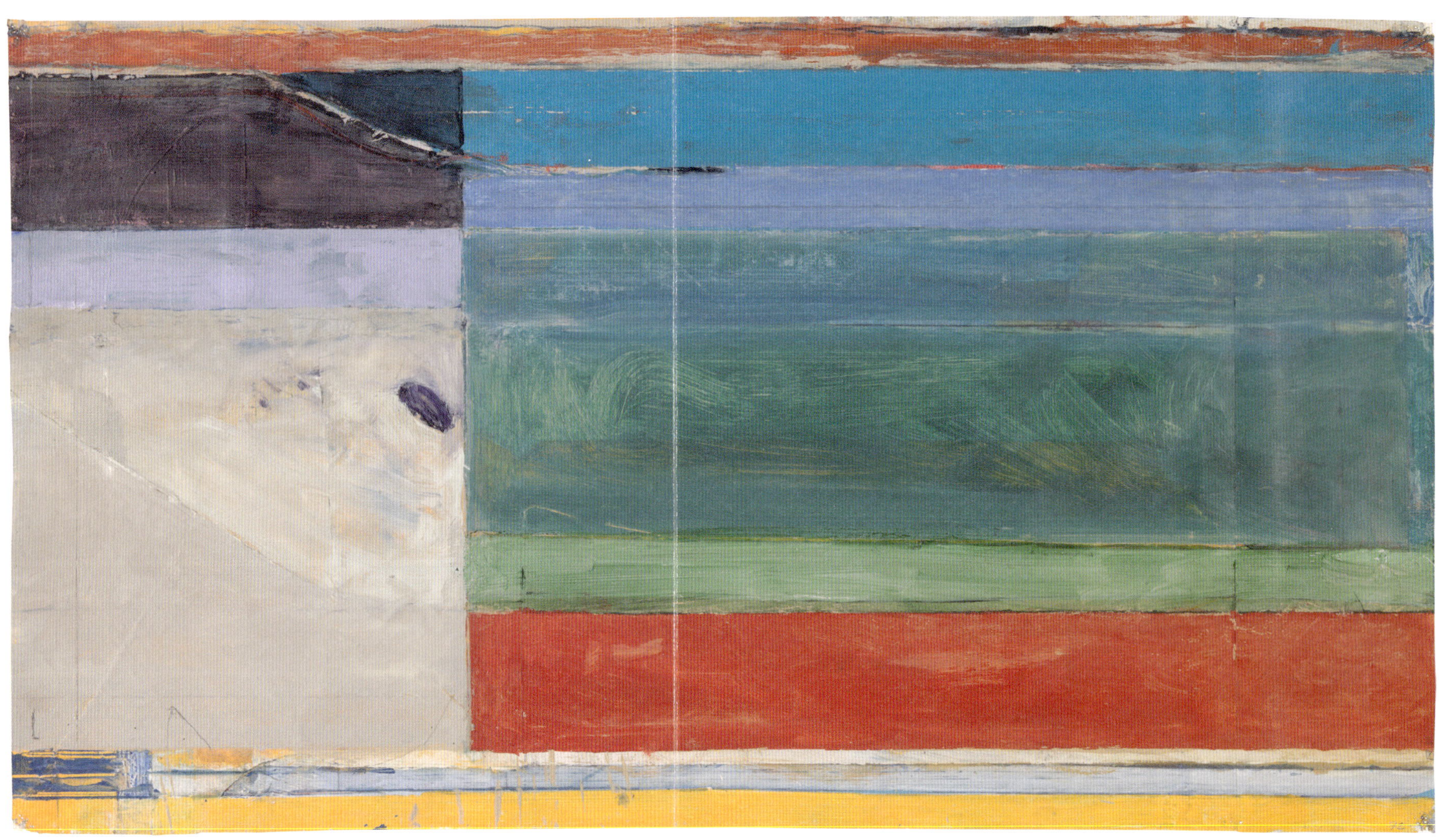

I came to mistrust my desire to explode the picture and super-charge it in some way... what is more important is a feeling of strength in reserve — tension beneath calm.

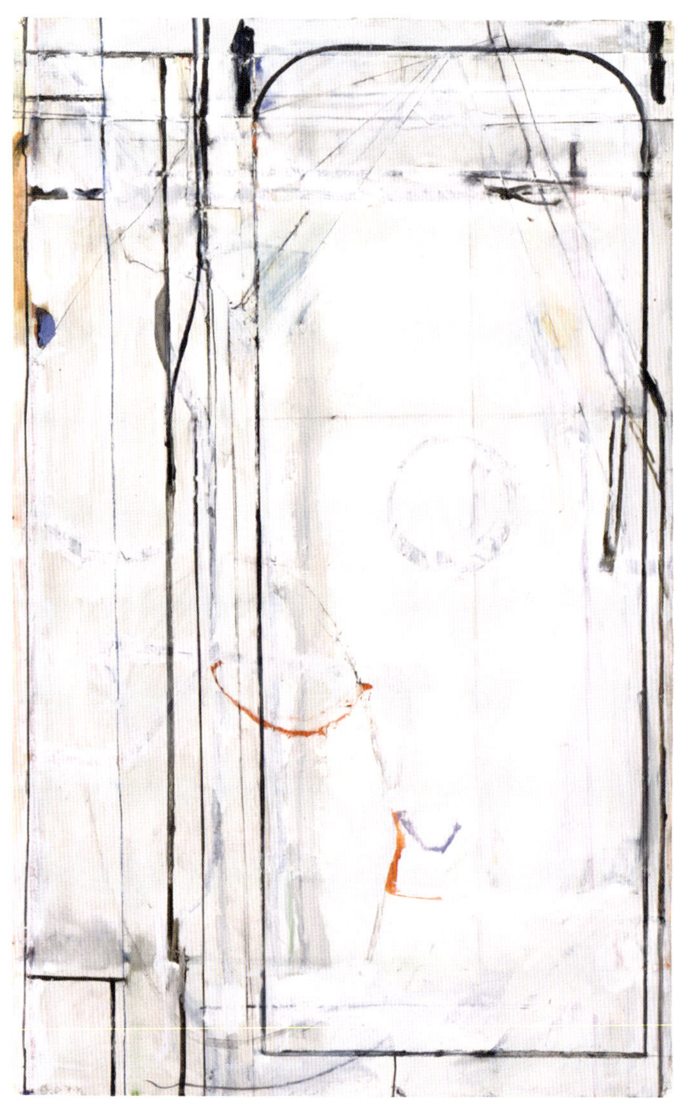

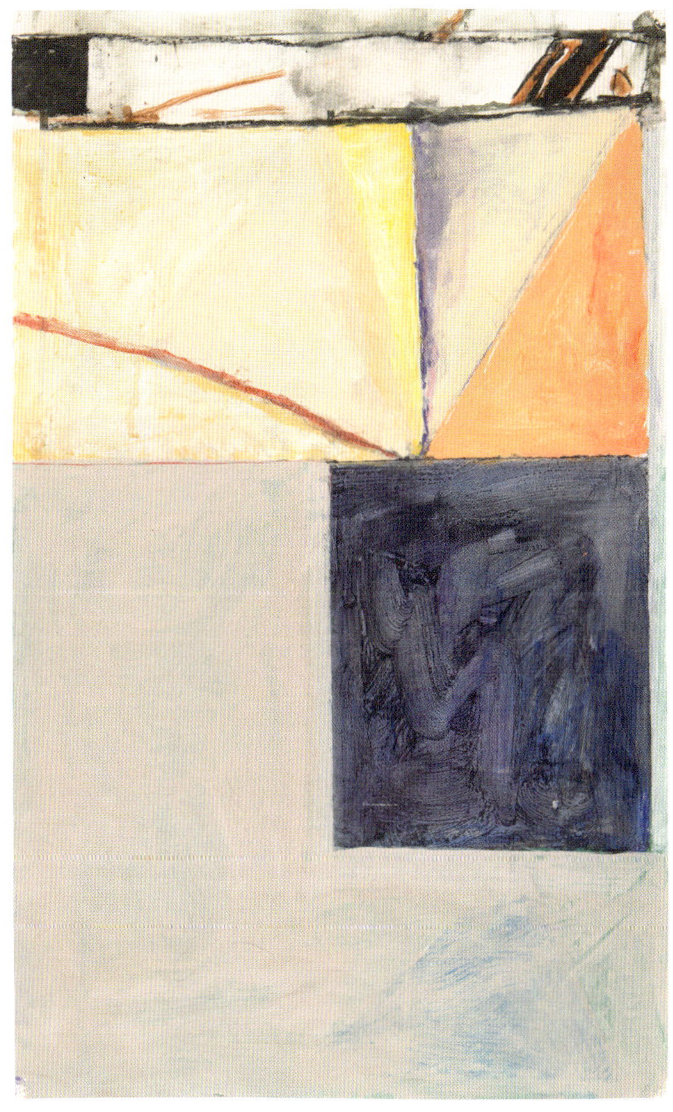

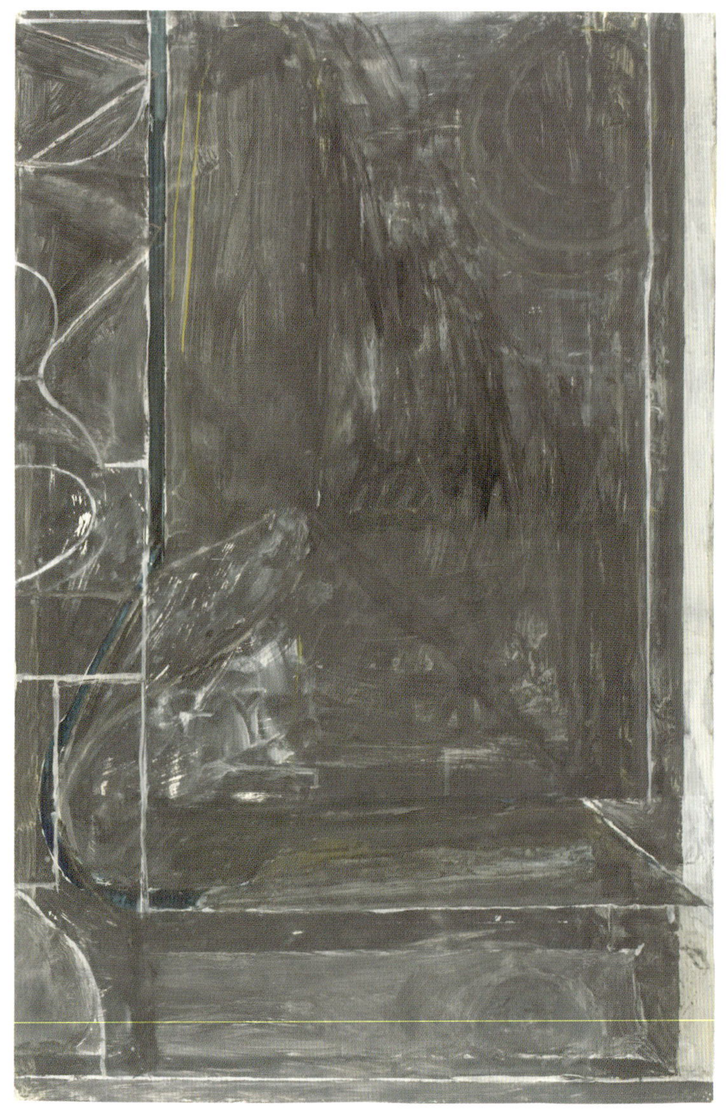

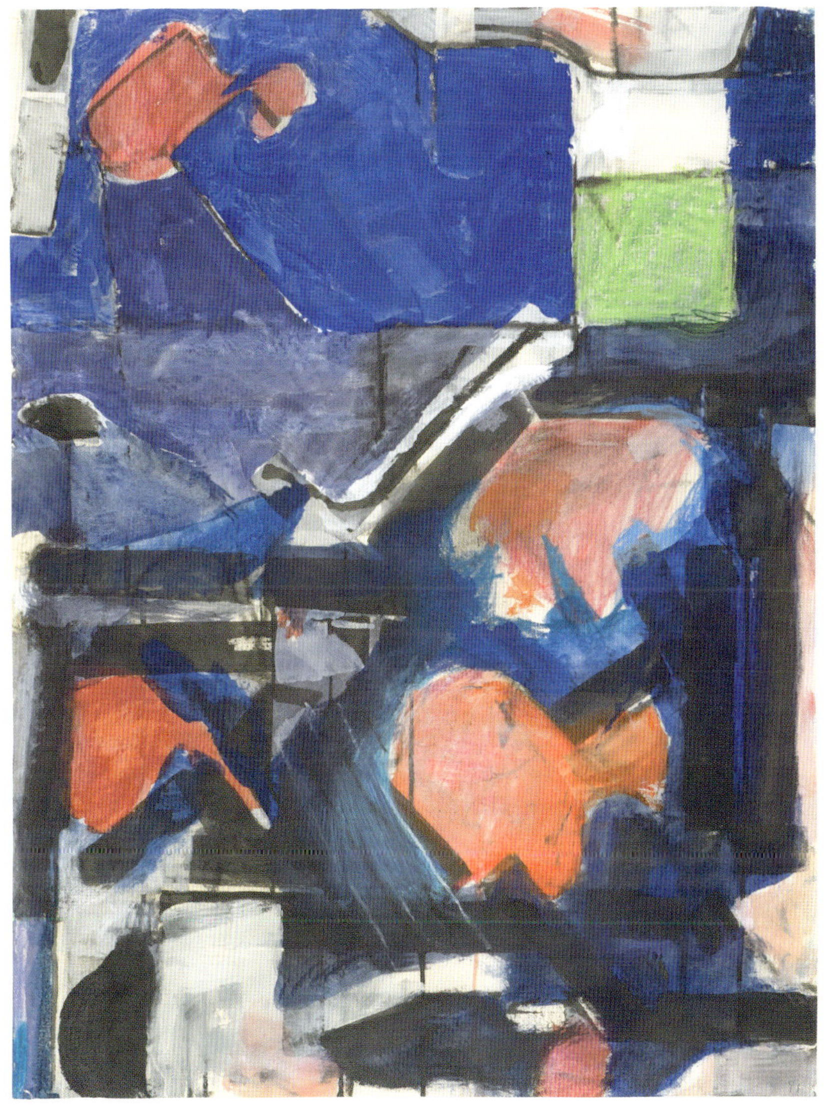

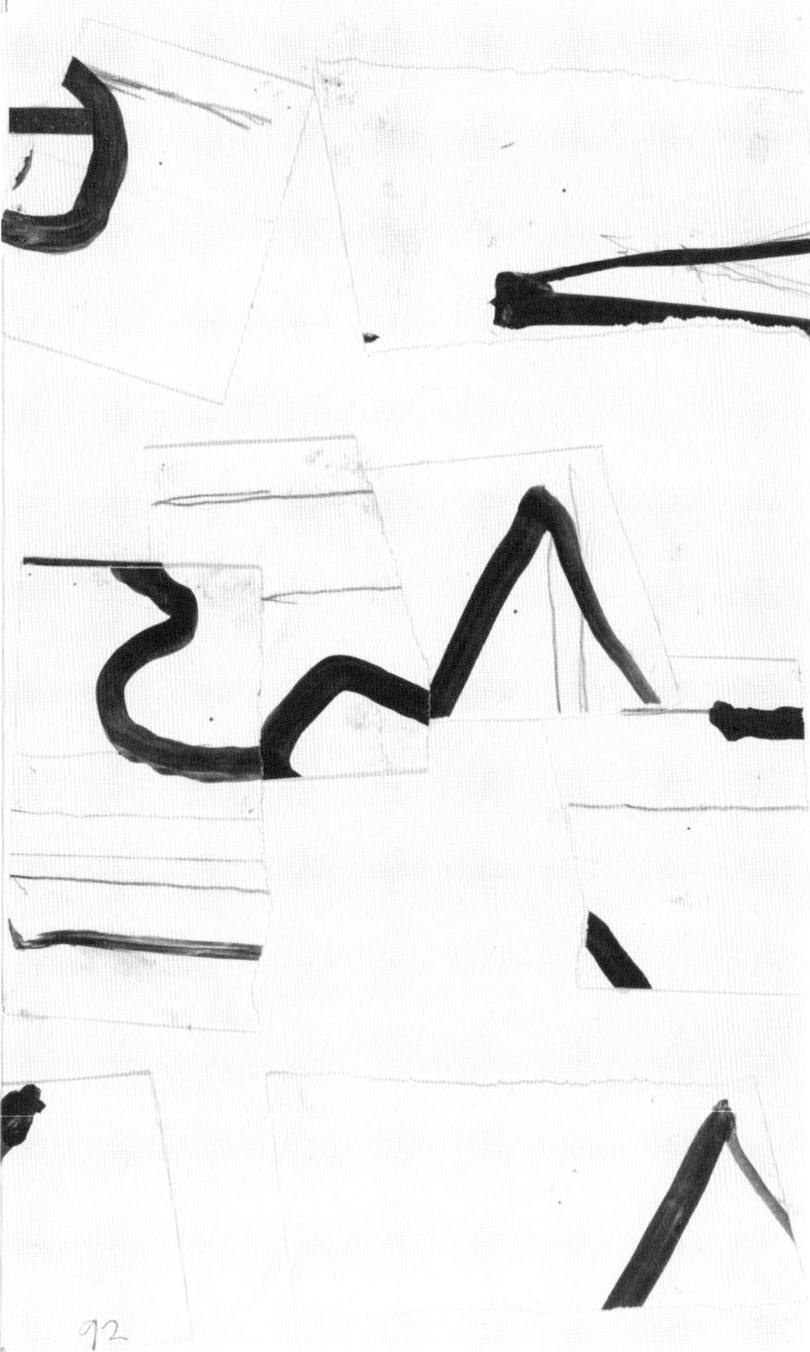
92

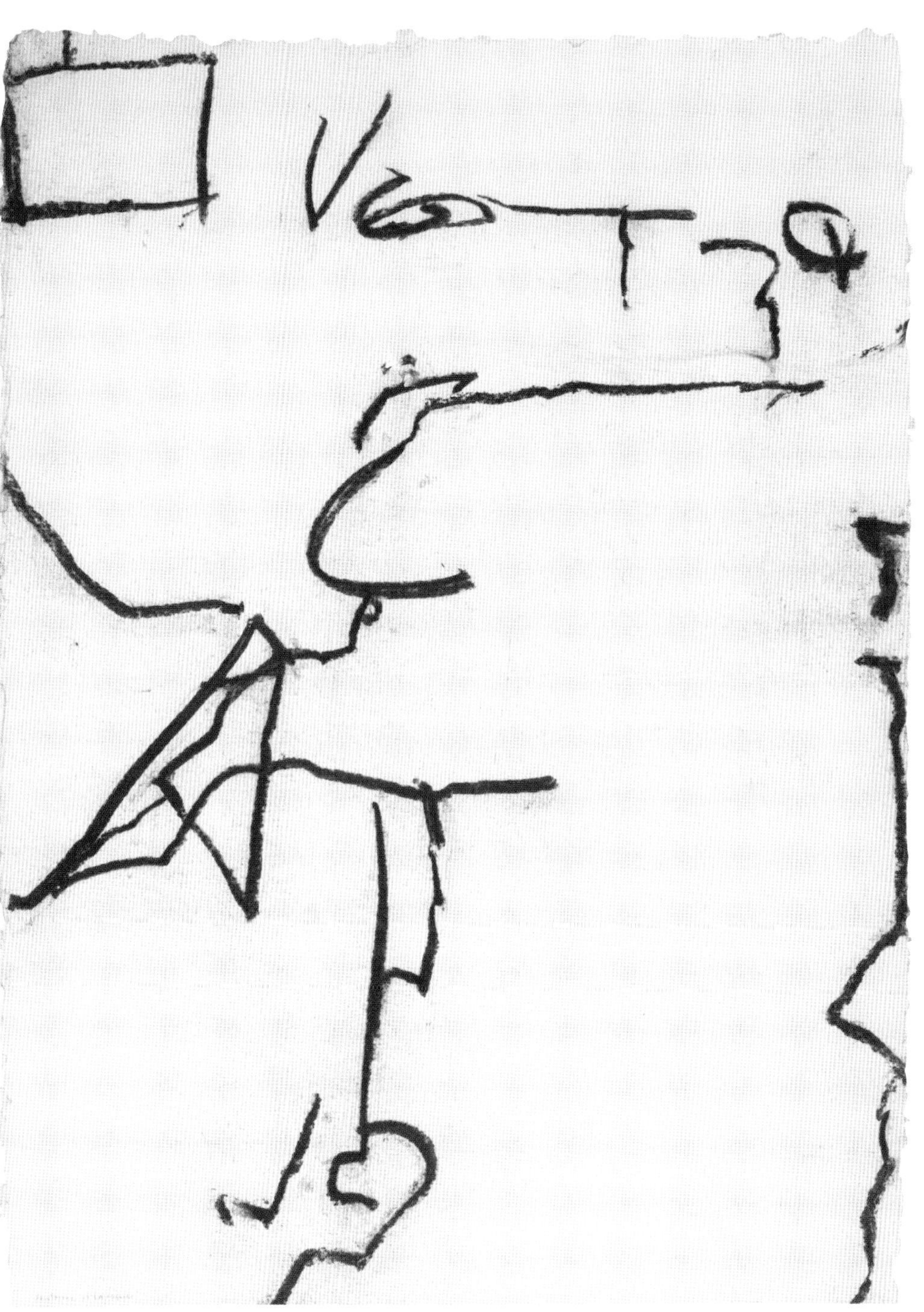

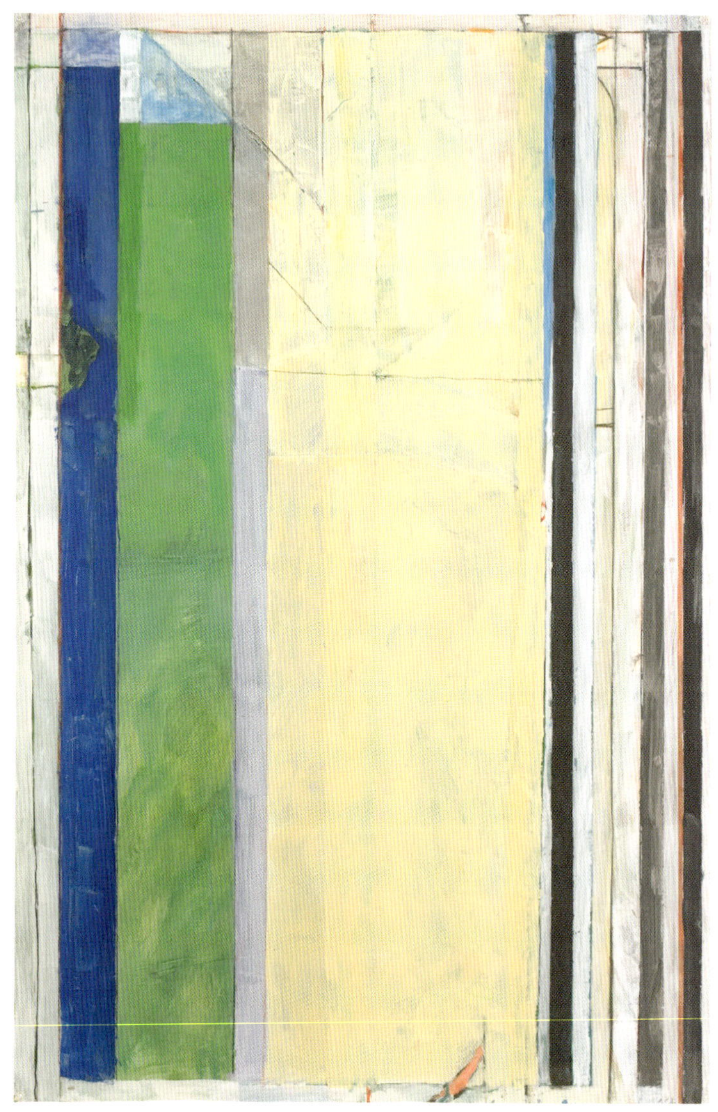

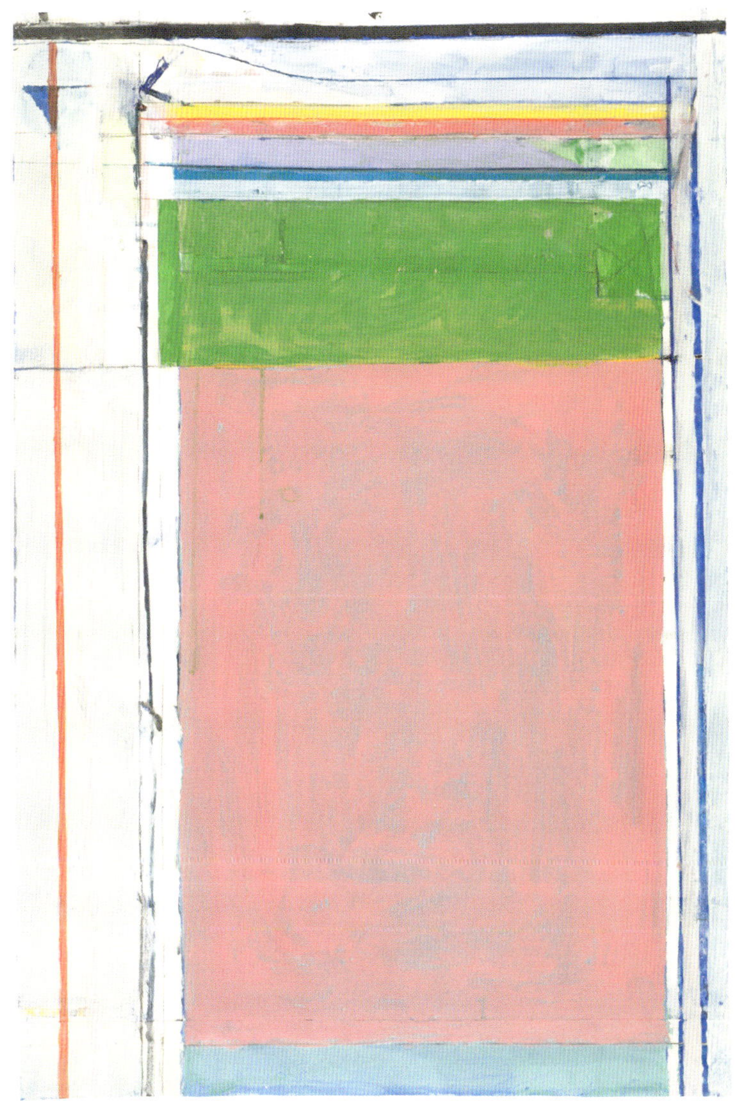

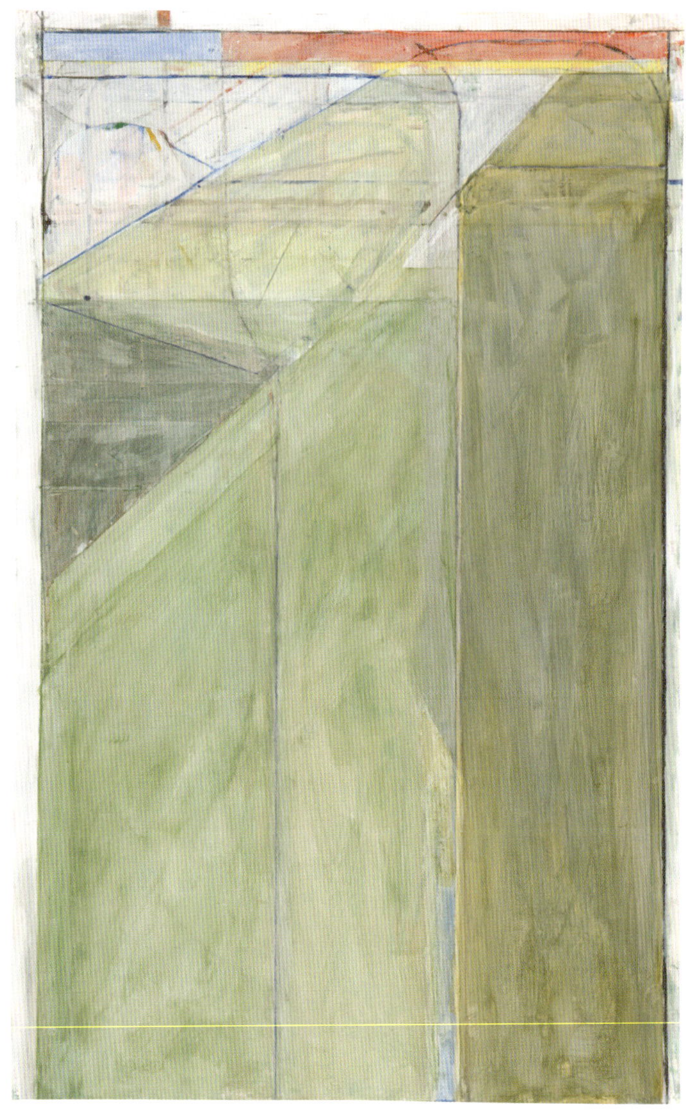

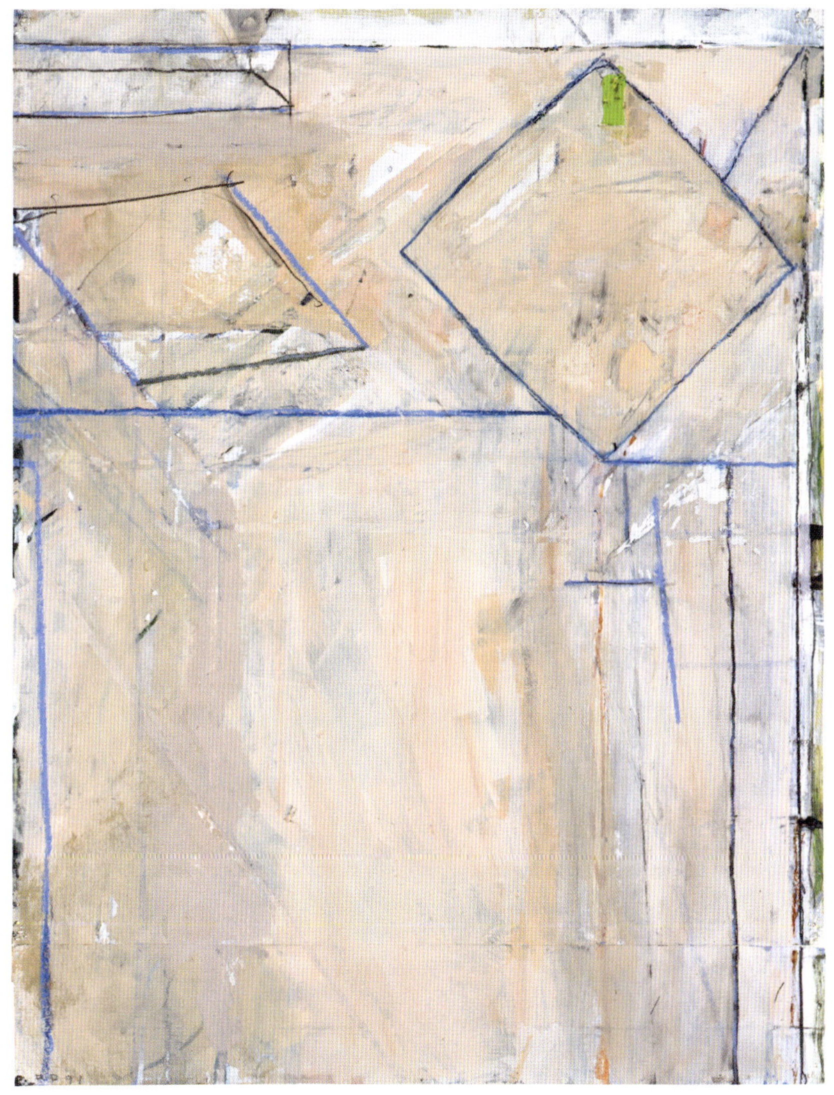

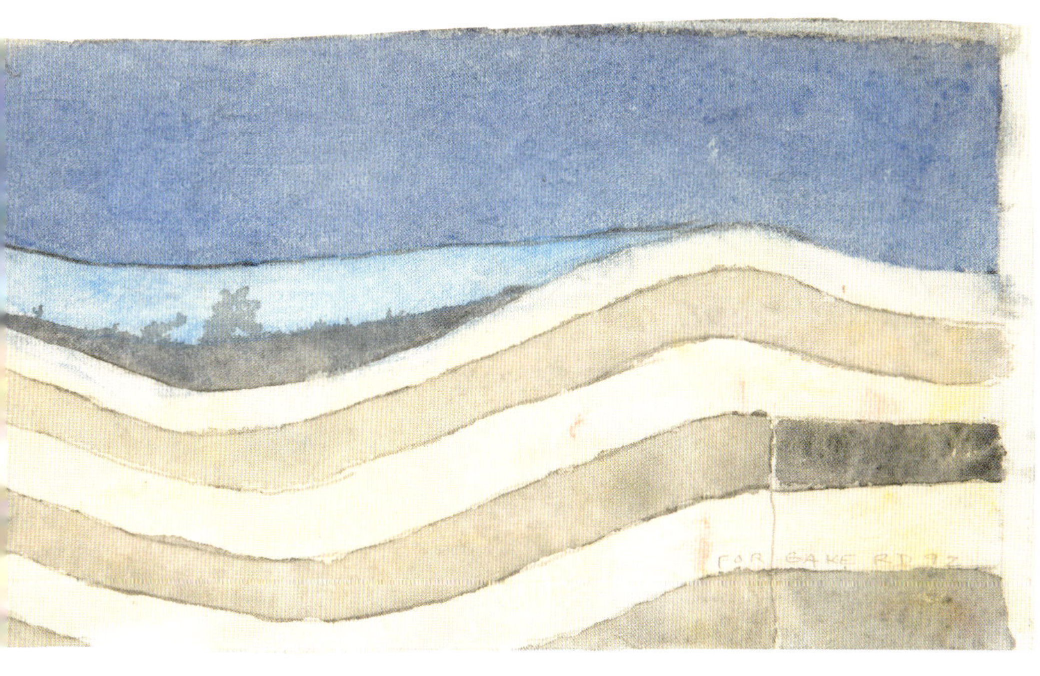
FOR GAKE RD 92

There is nothing I cannot paint over.

CATALOGUE CREDITS

Works included in "The Intimate Diebenkorn" tour are indicated by asterisks

Cover:
Untitled
1967/1991
Gouache, crayon, ballpoint pen, and graphite on paper
8 3/8 x 8 1/2 in. (21.3 x 21.6 cm)
Estate no. 2238

Page 4:
Untitled
c. 1950–55
Gouache and ink on paper
19 5/8 x 14 in. (49.8 x 35.6 cm)
Estate no. 2685V

Page 13:
Untitled
c. 1949–55
Gouache and ink on paper
11 x 8 1/2 in. (27.9 x 21.6 cm)
Estate no. 2652

Page 14 top:
Untitled
c. 1950–52
Gouache and ink on paper
14 x 17 in. (35.6 x 43.2 cm)
Estate no. 2656

Page 14 bottom:
Untitled
c. 1950–52
Gouache and ink on paper
14 x 17 in. (35.6 x 43.2 cm)
Estate no. 2655

Page 16:
*Untitled
c. 1949–52
Gouache, ink, and graphite on paper
16 3/4 x 13 3/4 in. (42.5 x 34.9 cm)
Estate no. 2689

Page 17:
Untitled
c. 1949–55
Gouache, graphite, and ink on paper
10 x 11 1/2 in. (25.4 x 29.2 cm)
Estate no. 2668R

Page 18:
*Untitled
1952
Ink and paper tape on joined paper
17 x 14 in. (43.2 x 35.6 cm)
Estate no. 3284

Page 19:
Untitled
c. 1949–55
Gouache and graphite on paper
14 x 11 in. (35.6 x 27.9 cm)
Estate no. 2663

Page 20:
*Untitled
c. 1949–55
Watercolor, graphite, and ink on paper
11 x 8 1/2 in. (27.9 x 21.6 cm)
Estate no. 2667

Page 21:
Untitled
c. 1950–52
Watercolor and graphite on paper
10 7/8 x 7 1/2 in. (27.6 x 19.1 cm)
Estate no. 2669R

Page 22:
Untitled
c. 1950–55
Ink and crayon on paper
16 7/8 x 13 7/8 in. (42.9 x 35.2 cm)
Estate no. 7588R

Page 23:
*Untitled
1952-53
Gouache on paper
17 x 14 in. (43.2 x 35.6 cm)
Estate no. 5502

Page 24:
Untitled
c. 1949–55
Gouache and graphite on paper
12 3/8 x 9 1/2 in. (31.4 x 24.1 cm)
Estate no. 2677

Page 25:
Untitled
c. 1949–55
Gouache and graphite on paper
8 3/8 x 7 in. (21.3 x 17.8 cm)
Estate no. 2675

Page 26 top:
*Untitled
c. 1949–55
Gouache and ink on paper
14 x 11 in. (35.6 x 27.9 cm)
Estate no. 3286

Page 26 bottom:
Untitled
c. 1950–55
Ink on paper
13 7/8 x 16 3/4 in. (35.2 x 42.5 cm)
Estate no. 7584

Page 28:
Untitled
1952
Ink and watercolor on paper
23 7/8 x 18 3/4 in. (60.6 x 47.6 cm)
Estate no. 7808

Page 29:
Untitled
1950
Ink and watercolor on paper
24 3/4 x 19 in. (62.9 x 48.3 cm)
Estate no. 7809R

Page 30:
Untitled
c. 1952–53
Gouache on paper
14 x 14 in. (35.6 x 35.6 cm)
Estate no. 5501

Page 31:
Untitled
c. 1952–53
Gouache on paper
17 x 14 in. (43.2 x 35.6 cm)
Estate no. 5498

Page 32:
Untitled
c. 1952–53
Watercolor and ink on cardboard
20 x 15 in. (50.8 x 38.1 cm)
Estate no. 3293

Page 33:
Untitled
1953
Gouache, graphite, and charcoal on paper
10 7/8 x 14 in. (27.6 x 35.6 cm)
Estate no. 2694

Page 34:
*Untitled
c. 1949–55
Gouache and ink on paper
13 x 8 1/2 in. (33 x 21.6 cm)
Estate no. 2682

Page 35:
Untitled
c. 1952–53
Ink and watercolor on paper
13 x 8 1/2 in. (33 x 21.6 cm)
Estate no. 5350

Page 36:
Untitled
c. 1949–55
Gouache and ink on paper
11 x 8 1/2 in. (27.9 x 21.6 cm)
Estate no. 2679

Page 37:
*Untitled
c. 1949–55
Watercolor and ink on paper
13 x 8 1/2 in. (33 x 21.6 cm)
Estate no. 2683

Page 38:
Untitled
c. 1952–53
Gouache on paper
17 1/8 x 14 in. (43.5 x 35.6 cm)
Estate no. 5351

Page 40 top:
Untitled
c. 1949–55
Gouache and ink on paper
8 1/2 x 11 in. (21.6 x 27.9 cm)
Estate no. 2654

Page 40 bottom:
Untitled
c. 1951–54
Gouache and ink on paper
12 1/2 x 18 7/8 in. (31.8 x 47.9 cm)
Estate no. 2686

Page 41:
Untitled
1956
Gouache and ink on paper mounted on cardboard
14 x 8 1/2 in. (35.6 x 21.6 cm)
Estate no. 3294

Page 42:
Untitled
c. 1950–55
Gouache and ink on paper
19 5/8 x 14 in. (49.8 x 35.6 cm)
Estate no. 2685R

Page 43:
Untitled
1949
Gouache on paper
24 x 18 in. (61 x 45.7 cm)
Estate no. 3219

Page 46:
*Untitled
1967–88
Gouache, charcoal, and ink on joined paper
18 5/8 x 13 3/4 in. (47.3 x 34.9 cm)
Estate no. 722R

Page 47:
*Untitled
1967–88
Gouache, ink, crayon, and graphite on paper
15 x 11 1/4 in. (38.1 x 28.6 cm)
Estate no. 2292

Page 48:
Untitled
1969
Ink on paper
16 x 13 3/4 in. (40.6 x 34.9 cm)
Estate no. 720

Page 49:
Untitled
1969
Ink on paper
15 x 11 1/4 in. (38.1 x 28.6 cm)
Estate no. 2307

Page 50 top:
Untitled
1969
Ink on paper
13 1/4 x 15 in. (33.7 x 38.1 cm)
Estate no. 2274R

Page 50 bottom:
Untitled
1969
Ink on paper
13 1/4 x 15 in. (33.7 x 38.1 cm)
Estate no. 2274V

Page 52:
Untitled
1970
Watercolor, acrylic, ink, charcoal, graphite, and pasted paper on paper
23 3/8 x 17 1/2 in. (59.4 x 44.5 cm)
Estate no. 159

Page 53:
Untitled
1971
Gouache on paper
28 1/2 x 22 1/2 in. (72.4 x 57.2 cm)
Estate no. 2309

Page 54:
Untitled
1971/1992
Cut-and-pasted paper, printed plastic, ink, and gouache on paper
23 7/8 x 18 in. (60.6 x 45.7 cm)
Estate no. 2265

Page 55:
Untitled
1973
Watercolor, graphite, and torn-and-pasted paper on paper
19 3/8 x 15 5/8 in. (49.2 x 39.7 cm)
Estate no. 60

Page 56:
Untitled
1972
Cut-and-pasted paper and acrylic on paper
21 1/2 x 17 in. (54.6 x 43.2 cm)
Estate no. 2353

Page 58:
Untitled
1978
Cut-and-pasted paper, manufactured colored paper, printed paper, gouache, and graphite on paper
13 1/4 x 9 1/4 in. (33.7 x 23.5 cm)
Estate no. 1604

Page 59:
Untitled (Collage)
1975
Acrylic, gouache, cut-and-pasted paper, and torn-and-pasted paper
11 3/4 x 8 1/2 in. (29.8 x 21.6 cm)
Estate no. 2213

Page 60:
*Untitled
c. 1975
Gouache on paper
24 x 18 3/4 in. (61 x 47.6 cm)
Estate no. 2318

Page 61:
Untitled
c. 1979
Gouache on paper
30 x 22 in. (76.2 x 55.9 cm)
Estate no. 2312

Page 63:
Untitled (Triptych)
1980
Gouache on paper
25 x 19 in. (63.5 x 48.3 cm)
Estate no. 2314

Page 65:
Untitled (Triptych)
1980
Gouache on paper
25 x 19 in. (63.5 x 48.3 cm)
Estate no. 2352

Page 66:
*Untitled (Spade)
c. 1981
Gouache on paper
12 7/8 x 12 1/2 in. (32.7 x 31.8 cm)
Estate no. 2348

Page 67:
Untitled #6
1981
Gouache, crayon, and graphite on paper
13 x 13 in. (33 x 33 cm)
Estate no. 3505

Page 68:
Untitled #23
1981
Gouache and crayon on paper
25 x 25 1/2 in. (63.5 x 64.8 cm)
Estate no. 187

Page 69:
Untitled #16
1981
Gouache and crayon on joined paper
24 x 25 in. (61 x 63.5 cm)
Estate no. 3510

Page 70:
Untitled
1981
Gouache on paper
25 x 19 in. (63.5 x 48.3 cm)
Estate no. 2341

Page 71:
Untitled
1981
Gouache and ink on paper
25 x 25 7/8 in. (63.5 x 65.7 cm)
Estate no. 2335

Page 72:
Untitled
1967–88
Gouache and graphite on joined paper
18 5/8 x 13 3/4 in. (47.3 x 34.9 cm)
Estate no. 722V

Page 73:
Untitled (Head)
1982
Watercolor and charcoal on paper
17 x 14 in. (43.2 x 35.6 cm)
Estate no. 2083

Page 74:
Untitled
1985
Cut-and-pasted paper, graphite, wax, and cut-and-pasted printed paper on paper
7 x 5 in. (17.8 x 12.7 cm)
Estate no. 2547

Page 75:
Untitled
1985
Collage of vellum, construction paper, acrylic, pastel and graphite on board
11 3/4 x 8 1/2 in. (29.8 x 21.6 cm)
Estate no. 5894

Page 76:
Untitled (Ocean Park)
1987
Acrylic, gouache, and crayon on paper
38 x 25 in. (96.5 x 63.5 cm)
Estate no. 2448

Page 81:
*Untitled
c. 1988–92
Gouache, pasted paper, graphite, and crayon on paper
9 1/2 x 6 5/16 in. (24.1 x 16 cm)
Estate no. 2503

Page 82:
Untitled
1992
Cut-and-pasted paper, gouache, and graphite on paper
13 1/2 x 13 7/8 in. (34.3 x 35.2 cm)
Estate no. 2510

Page 83:
Untitled
c. 1988–92
Gouache, crayon, and pasted paper on joined paper
32 x 22 in. (81.3 x 55.9 cm)
Estate no. 2507

Page 84:
Untitled
c. 1988–92
Graphite, gouache, and ink on paper
12 x 9 in. (30.5 x 22.9 cm)
Estate no. 2506

Page 85:
Untitled
c. 1988–92
Gouache, ink, and graphite on paper
15 x 14 in. (38.1 x 35.6 cm)
Estate no. 2254

Page 87:
Untitled
c. 1988
Ink, gouache, crayon, and graphite on paper
12 x 9 in. (30.5 x 22.9 cm)
Estate no. 5793

Page 88:
Untitled
1984/1992
Acrylic, gouache, crayon, and graphite on paper
38 x 25 in. (96.5 x 63.5 cm)
Estate no. 2205

Page 89:
Untitled #17
1989
Crayon, graphite, and gouache on paper
30 1/4 x 23 in. (76.8 x 58.4 cm)
Estate no. 2426

Page 90:
Soda Rock I
1988
Cut-and-pasted paper, torn-and-pasted paper, crayon, gouache, fabric, and plastic on paper
12 3/4 x 9 in. (32.4 x 22.9 cm)
Estate no. 2321

Page 91:
Untitled
1989
Gouache, acrylic, pasted paper, graphite, and crayon on paper
12 1/2 x 9 3/8 in. (31.8 x 23.8 cm)
Estate no. 2225

Page 92:
Untitled #12
1989–91
Crayon, graphite, and acrylic on paper
38 x 25 in. (96.5 x 63.5 cm)
Estate no. 2425

Page 93:
Untitled #11
1990
Crayon, graphite, gouache, and cut-and-pasted paper on joined paper
33 3/4 x 25 in. (85.7 x 63.5 cm)
Estate no. 2429

Page 94:
Untitled #19
1990
Crayon, graphite, acrylic, gouache, and pasted paper on paper backed with linen
23 1/4 x 17 3/4 in. (59.1 x 45.1 cm)
Estate no. 2431

Page 95:
Untitled #4
1991
Crayon, graphite, gouache, and pasted paper on paper
30 1/4 x 23 in. (76.8 x 58.4 cm)
Estate no. 2430

Gatefold front:
Untitled #10
1991
Acrylic, crayon, and graphite on joined paper
22 x 39 5/8 in. (55.9 x 100.6 cm)
Estate no. 2268

Gatefold reverse:
Untitled
1992
Acrylic, graphite, and cut-and-pasted paper
19 x 34 in. (48.3 x 86.4 cm)
Estate no. 2259

Page 98:
Untitled #9
1988
Oil, acrylic, crayon, graphite, and pasted paper on paper
32 x 20 in. (81.3 x 50.8 cm)
Estate no. 2424

Page 99:
Untitled
c. 1988–92
Gouache and crayon on paper
24 1/2 x 18 in. (62.2 x 45.7 cm)
Estate no. 2247

Page 100:
Untitled #2
1991
Crayon, acrylic, and gouache on paper
37 3/4 x 25 in. (95.9 x 63.5 cm)
Estate no. 2433

Page 101:
Untitled
1991
Acrylic, charcoal, and gouache on paper
25 x 19 in. (63.5 x 48.3 cm)
Estate no. 2222

Page 102:
*Untitled
1992
Cut-and-pasted paper, torn-and-pasted paper, ink, and graphite on paper
13 x 7 3/4 in. (33 x 19.7 cm)
Estate no. 2250

Page 105:
Untitled
c. 1988–92
Charcoal on handmade "Hawthorne of Larroque" paper
34 x 23 1/4 in. (86.4 x 59.1 cm)
Estate no. 2249

Page 106:
Untitled
1992
Gouache and graphite ††on paper
37 3/4 x 25 in. (95.9 x 63.5 cm)
Estate no. 2221

Page 107:
Untitled
1992
Gouache, crayon, and graphite on joined paper
39 x 26 1/4 in. (99.1 x 66.7 cm)
Estate no. 2322

Page 108:
Untitled #13
1991
Crayon, graphite, gouache, and cut-and-pasted paper on paper
37 7/8 x 23 7/8 in. (96.2 x 60.6 cm)
Estate no. 2432

Page 109:
Untitled #7
1991
Crayon, graphite, acrylic, and cut-and-pasted paper on paper
20 1/2 x 16 in. (52.1 x 40.6 cm)
Estate no. 2427

Page 111:
Untitled
1992
Gouache on paper
6 x 10 in. (15.2 x 25.4 cm)
Estate no. 201

TEXT CREDITS

Page 15:
"A way is just what I don't want..." Richard Diebenkorn, quoted in *Temperaments: Artists Facing Their Work* by Dan Hofstadter (New York: Knopf, 1992), p. 176.

Page 27:
"I can never accomplish what I want..." Richard Diebenkorn, quoted in a miscellaneous studio note in *Richard Diebenkorn* by Gerald Nordland (New York: Rizzoli International Publications, 1987), p. 89.

Page 39:
"It wasn't art that I was interested in..." Richard Diebenkorn, quoted in "Tape recorded interview with Richard Diebenkorn, May 1, 1985" by Susan Larsen. Archives of American Art, Smithsonian Institution, Washington, DC.

Page 51:
"One wants to see the artifice..." Richard Diebenkorn, quoted in *Contemporary Bay Area Figurative Painting*, Paul Mills, ed. (Oakland Art Museum, 1957), p. 12.

Page 77:
"I'm not comfortable being..." Richard Diebenkorn, quoted in "Tape recorded interview with Richard Diebenkorn, May 7, 1985" by Susan Larsen. Archives of American Art, Smithsonian Institution, Washington, DC.

Page 97:
"I came to mistrust..." Richard Diebenkorn, quoted in *Contemporary Bay Area Figurative Painting*, Paul Mills, ed. (Oakland Art Museum, 1957), p. 12.

Page 113:
"There is nothing I cannot paint over." Richard Diebenkorn, quoted in *Temperaments: Artists Facing Their Work* by Dan Hofstadter (New York: Knopf, 1992), p. 193.

RICHARD DIEBENKORN

Richard Diebenkorn, born in Portland, Oregon, in 1922, grew up in San Francisco. He attended Stanford University, where he studied art and met his wife, Phyllis. After a period in the Marine Corps during WWII, Diebenkorn continued his study of art at the California School of Fine Arts in San Francisco. In 1947, he was hired as an instructor at the CSFA, which from 1946–1950 was the center of Abstract Expressionism on the west coast.

Diebenkorn continued to pursue abstraction after leaving the Bay Area in 1950 while working for his MA at the University of New Mexico in Albuquerque, later as assistant professor at the University of Illinois in Urbana during 1952, and after returning to Berkeley in 1953.

After the enormously productive Berkeley series of paintings, Diebenkorn turned to the figure. Once a week, from about 1955–1966, Diebenkorn and a group of artists that included David Park, Elmer Bischoff, and Frank Lobdell gathered in each other's studios to draw from the model. Often identified together as Bay Area Figurative artists, they applied Abstract Expressionist methods to representational subjects.

Drawn back into abstraction after moving to Southern California in 1966 to teach at UCLA, Diebenkorn began his most sustained and renowned period, during which he created the Ocean Park series. He also worked intensely on his works on paper.

During the last few years of Diebenkorn's life, he and Phyllis returned to Northern California. The drawings he made while living in rural Alexander Valley were marked by complexity and ambition. Diebenkorn died in 1993.

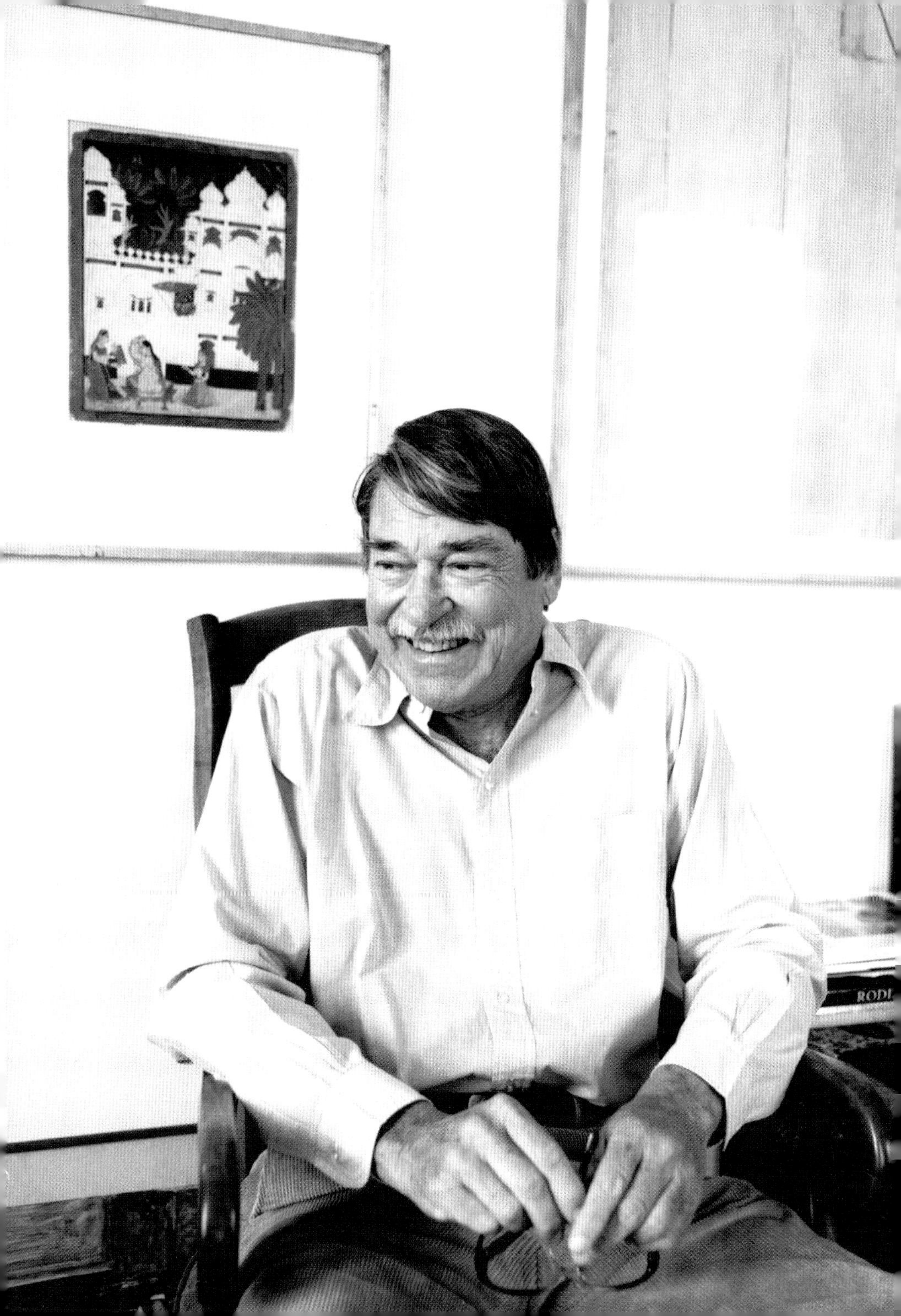

EDITOR'S NOTE

The editor wishes to thank the Richard Diebenkorn Foundation for allowing us to select images from the master's extraordinary archive for this book. A special thanks to Richard Grant, Andrea Liguori, Daisy Murray Holman, and Carl Schmitz of the Foundation for providing assistance every step of the way. Thanks also to Chester Arnold, a true partner in this project, for his wise counsel during the selection of these images.

COLOPHON

Published by Kelly's Cove Press

June 2013

Typefaces

Linotype Didot by Adrian Frutiger

Sabon by Jan Tschichold

Printing and Binding

Versa Press, Inc.

East Peoria, Illinois

Drawings

Richard Diebenkorn

Photographs of Drawings

Courtesy of

the Richard Diebenkorn Foundation

Design

Vincent Romero

Robin Ann McIntosh

ALSO FROM KELLY'S COVE PRESS

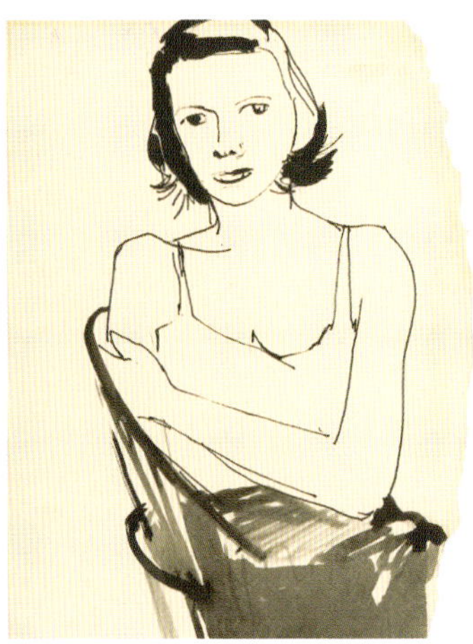

After a distinguished early career as an abstract painter, Richard Diebenkorn (1922–1993) focused primarily on the human figure from the mid-1950s to the early 1960s. With noted Bay Area painters David Park, Elmer Bischoff, Theophilus Brown, and Frank Lobdell, Diebenkorn drew regularly from live models. In his introduction to this volume, Sonoma painter Chester Arnold says, "[Diebenkorn] rarely paid academic homage to anatomy, yet the accuracy of his readings yields that rare fusion of knowing and questioning, of grace and impetuousness that give his drawings their dignity and power." Of the 99 images reproduced in this volume, most are previously unpublished and available here for the first time.

$20.00

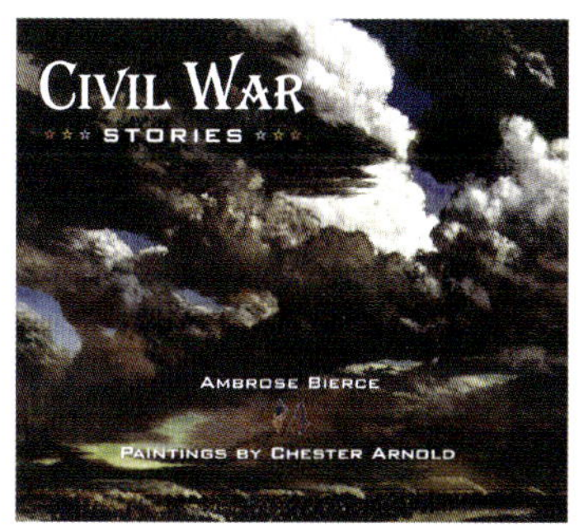

Ambrose Bierce's classic series of Civil War stories is paired here with stunning paintings by Sonoma realist master Chester Arnold. Bierce's understated narrative technique—a disengaged voice opposite powerfully graphic imagery—anticipates Hemingway by more than a generation, while Arnold's paintings reflect on the hollow devastation that human violence leaves behind.

$25.00

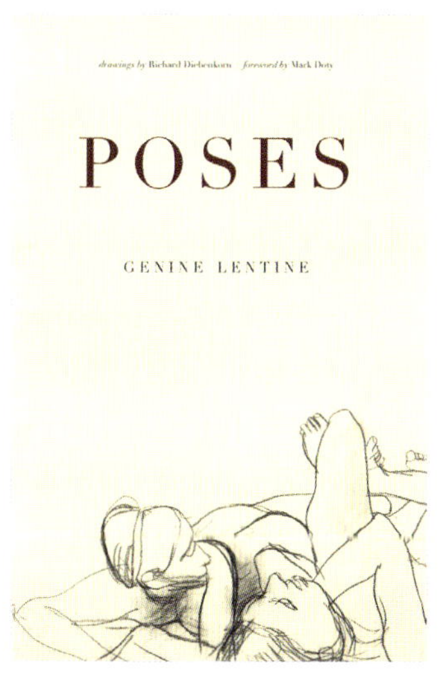

Collected here with figure drawings by Richard Diebenkorn are Lentine's most poignant gestures, which exist as part of an ongoing inquiry into what we see when we regard the body.

"Luminously intelligent... *Poses* is something we haven't seen. About how many books can that genuinely be said? Sly, artful, restless, this fresh and lovely thing invites us to awaken, again, to the body, to the struggle to see what's in front of us, to pleasure, to the world."
— Mark Doty, from the foreword

$20.00

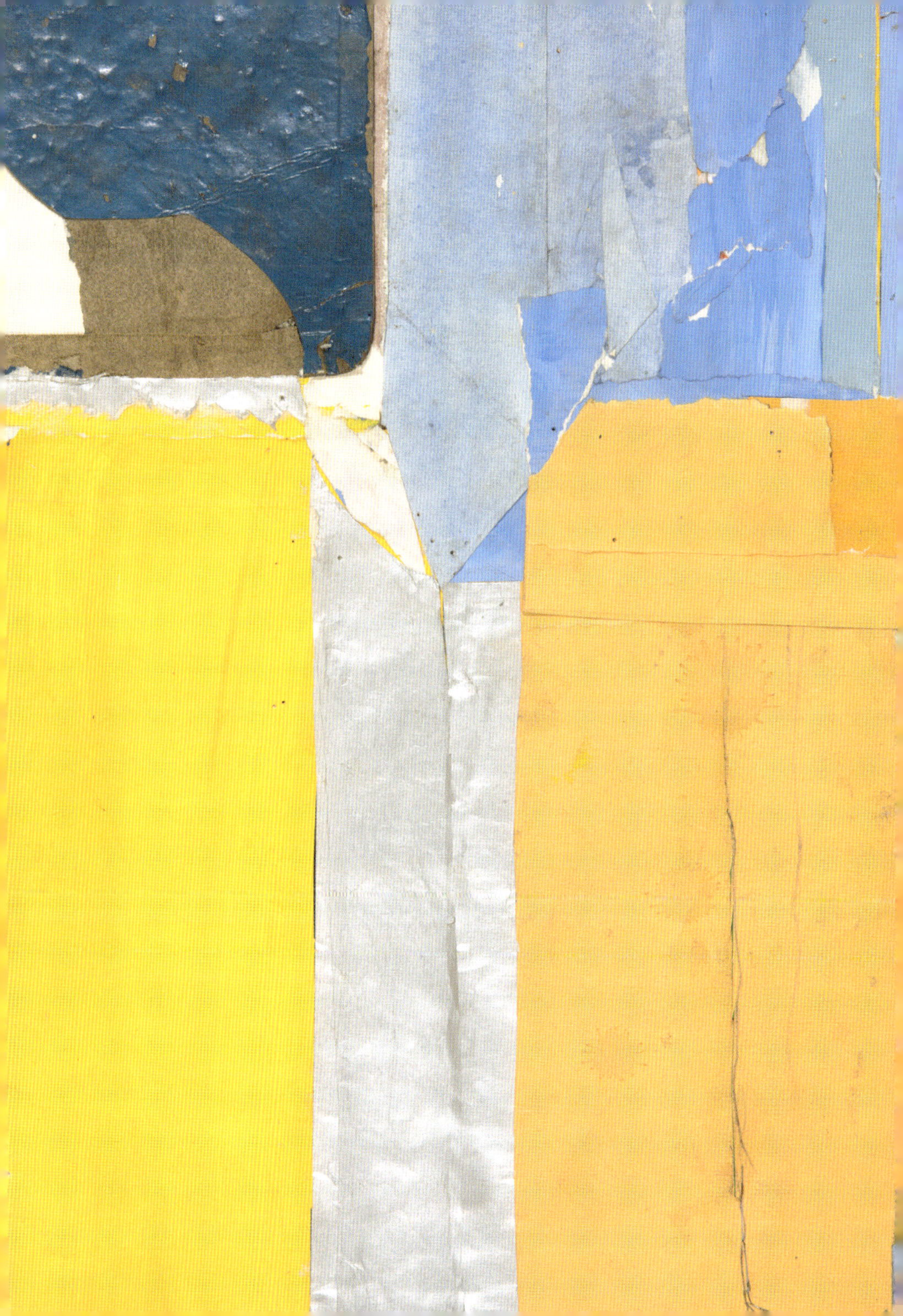

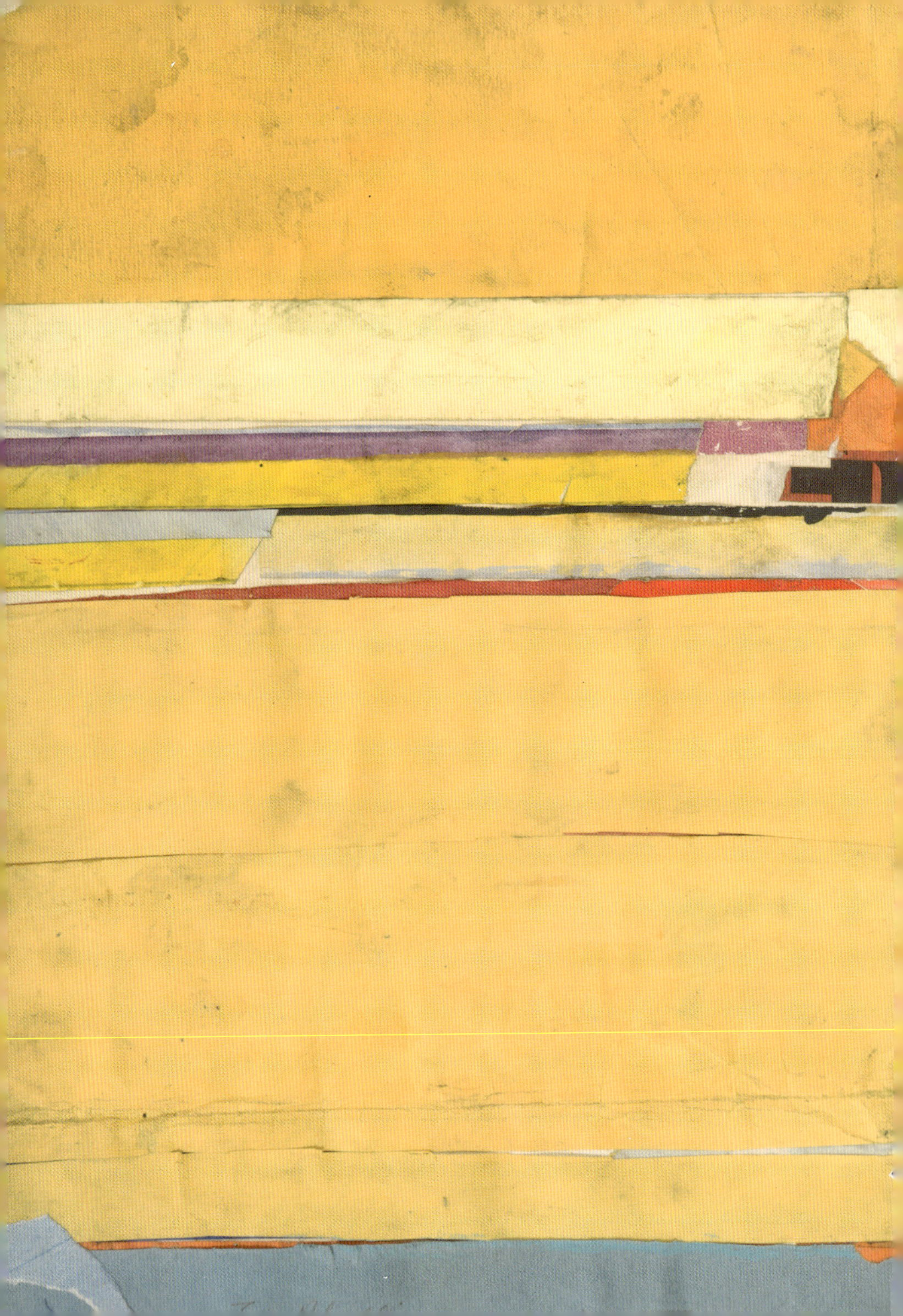